FOUNDATIONS OF MODERN POLITICAL SCIENCE SERIES

Robert A. Dahl, Editor

THE AGE OF IDEOLOGY—POLITICAL THOUGHT, 1750 TO THE PRESENT, Second Edition
by Frederick M. Watkins

THE AMERICAN PARTY SYSTEM AND THE AMERICAN PEOPLE, Second Edition
by Fred I. Greenstein

THE ANALYSIS OF INTERNATIONAL RELATIONS
by Karl W. Deutsch

COMPARATIVE GOVERNMENT
by Dankwart A. Rustow

CONGRESS AND THE PRESIDENCY, Second Edition
by Nelson W. Polsby

INTEREST-GROUPS
by Graham Wootton

JUDICIAL BEHAVIOR
by David J. Danelski

MODERN POLITICAL ANALYSIS, Second Edition
by Robert A. Dahl

PERSPECTIVES IN CONSTITUTIONAL LAW, with Revisions
by Charles L. Black, Jr.

THE POLICY-MAKING PROCESS
by Charles E. Lindblom

POLITICS AND POLICIES IN STATE AND LOCAL GOVERNMENTS
by Herbert Kaufman

PUBLIC ADMINISTRATION
by James W. Fesler

PUBLIC OPINION
by Robert E. Lane and David O. Sears

SYSTEMS OF POLITICAL SCIENCE
by Oran R. Young

READINGS IN AMERICAN POLITICAL BEHAVIOR, Second Edition
edited by Raymond E. Wolfinger

READINGS IN INTERNATIONAL POLITICAL BEHAVIOR
edited by Naomi Rosenbaum

READINGS IN MODERN POLITICAL ANALYSIS
edited by Robert A. Dahl and Deane E. Neubauer

READINGS ON STATE AND LOCAL GOVERNMENT
edited by Irwin N. Gertzog

FOUNDATIONS OF MODERN POLITICAL SCIENCE SERIES

PRENTICE-HALL, INC., Englewood Cliffs, New Jersey

INTEREST-GROUPS

GRAHAM WOOTTON

Tufts University

FOUNDATIONS OF MODERN POLITICAL SCIENCE SERIES

Robert A. Dahl, Editor

INTEREST-GROUPS
by Graham Wootton

© 1970 by PRENTICE-HALL, INC., Englewood Cliffs, New Jersey. All rights reserved. No part of this book may be reproduced in any form or by any means without permission in writing from the publisher. Printed in the United States of America. Library of Congress Catalog Card No.: 77–89819.

Design by John J. Dunleavy

(p)   13–469239–X   (c)   13–469247–O

PRENTICE-HALL INTERNATIONAL, INC., London
PRENTICE-HALL OF AUSTRALIA, PTY. LTD., Sydney
PRENTICE-HALL OF CANADA, LTD., Toronto
PRENTICE-HALL OF INDIA PRIVATE LTD., New Delhi
PRENTICE-HALL OF JAPAN, INC., Tokyo

Current printing (last number):

10   9   8   7   6   5   4   3   2   1

For Mary

PREFACE

If you are looking for "the facts" about interest-groups (numbers, distribution, etc.), this is not the place to find them. What I first attempt is to clear up that muddle over terms and definitions which at present allows, for instance, "pressure group," "lobby," and "interest-group" to be given different meanings by different writers. If you follow me in the attempt, you will get two things for the price of one: you will learn not only about the subject ("the facts" in the more important sense of *relationships*) but also about handling problems of definition and of the choice and formation of concepts. Initially I invite you to set aside the inconsistent terms and notions and to inquire what sort of thing this thing *interest-group* really is. This procedure was for long known as real definition; it is invoked here, ultimately as a teaching device, in three of its forms: abstraction (and naming), analysis, and synthesis. That takes up Chapters Two and Three, where I also outline a new classification of interest-groups based upon a modified functionalism. This classification purports to be "meaningful" rather than "logical," i.e., to explain the observed actions (or behavior) of such groups rather than merely to reduce them to manageable order.

In Chapter Four I try to explain the different styles of action that interest-groups exhibit, provisionally making use, as immediate determinants, of five sets of compound variables. I then tackle another muddle: that in which the discussion of the influence (or power) of interest-groups too often finds itself. Adapting distinctions derived from Professor Robert Dahl earlier in this series, I suggest four possible indicators of interest-group influence and draw out their "operational" implications—what we should do when comparing the influence of different groups in order, paradoxically, to keep *in*comparability within tolerable limits of error. Deciding to allow ourselves to say that some interest-groups *are* more influential than others, we go on to inquire into the reasons for such differences. Finally I draw attention to some closely related flows of influence upon public policy, and ask how far these observations require us to modify the concept used in the preceding chapters.

Debts are not always easy to identify, much less repay, but I am conscious that Professor Joseph LaPalombara helped me in the most generous way possible. Professor Samuel Beer, when told that I had been commissioned to write this volume, promptly advised me to try my hand "at some theory," which was just the encouragement I needed "to travel hopefully" in that general direction—"a better thing than to arrive," or so Robert Louis Stevenson would have us believe. I am grateful for the help of James J. Murray, Roger G. Emblen, and Cecil Yarbrough at Prentice-Hall. My main debt is to my academic editor, Professor Robert Dahl, who gave generously of his advice, encouragement, and hospitality at New Haven. After the book had been written, his advice was again sought and readily given. I thank him for that, and for giving me my opportunity—and my head—in the first place.

Graham Wootton

Warborough, Oxford

1969

CONTENTS

CHAPTER ONE

DEFINITIONS ABOUNDING

page 1   Of interest group, pressure group, lobby and lobbying. Definitions of words (nominal) and of things (real). Three types of real definition: abstraction, analysis, synthesis. Real definitions of interest group.

CHAPTER TWO

ABSTRACTION AND NAMING

page 6   Abstraction not confined to "observables" but entails attribution by observer of social meaning to "raw" behavior he observes. The two-step process of abstraction. The abstractions (reconstructed) to which the words "lobby" and "interest group" refer. The derivative concept, Interest-Group.

CHAPTER THREE

ANALYSIS, SYNTHESIS, CLASSIFICATION

page 20   Analysis of the interest-group concept into its component parts. Synthesis: interest-groups as components of a type of society. Classifying groups by social contribution (using Parsonian "pattern variables") and "levels": first-order, second-order, third-order. Core-groups and peripheral groups (ascribed and achieved).

CHAPTER FOUR

DETERMINANTS OF STYLES OF ACTION

page 45   Ultimate as against immediate determinants. A provisional set of immediate (compound) variables. Use of these for intersystem comparisons. Short-run and long-run analyses.

CHAPTER FIVE

THE INFLUENCE OF INTEREST-GROUPS

page 73   That relationship of interest-group to government which is denoted by "influence." Possible indicators of interest-group influence. The "operational" procedures implied in the indicators. Determinants of influence.

CHAPTER SIX

THE MULTIPLE FLOW OF INFLUENCE

page 96   Some qualifications: flow of influence may not be "simplex" (or one-way) but "duplex" (in reverse), or "simplex-duplex" combined (as in "quadruple plays"). "Self-contained" flows within area of government itself. Significance of these qualifications for the interest-group concept.

TO EXPLORE FURTHER

page 103

INDEX

page 109

INTEREST-GROUPS

CHAPTER ONE

DEFINITIONS ABOUNDING

"Interest group" forms part of a cluster of terms that includes "pressure group" and "lobby" at the center and "organized group," "private organization," and "catalytic group" at the circumference. If such profusion may be charitably interpreted as a sign of the vitality of political science, it nonetheless makes for confusion, at least in the minds of the student and the general reader. As evidence consider no more than the following:

[1] [Interest groups are] all groups or associations which seek to influence public policy in their own chosen direction, while declining to accept direct responsibility for ruling the country.

[2] [A pressure group is] any organization which seeks to influence government policy without at the same time being willing to accept the responsibility of public office.

[3a] [An interest group] is a shared-attitude group that makes certain claims upon other groups in the society.

[3b] If and when [an interest group] makes its claims through or upon any of the institutions of government, it becomes a political interest group.

[4] When interest groups act at the political level, they are called pressure groups.

[5] Interest group is used interchangeably with pressure group.

[6] Lobbying means men acting to influence government decisions.
. . .

[7] [Lobbying is] besetting and worrying members of legislatures with persuasions to vote for or against a bill. . . .

1

Now go back to the beginning and read horizontally. Quotations 1 and 2 are from the British scholars S. E. Finer and N. C. Hunt[1] respectively. They describe the same notion or activity, almost (by chance) in identical words, but they use different names. Vertically, set Finer against the American David Truman (item 3a), author of a landmark book on the subject[2]; same name ("interest group"), but a different notion or activity. Or contrast Truman in 3b with Jean-Daniel Reynaud[3] in 4—same notion or activity (apparently), but different names. It would not be surprising if you now clutched desperately at the straw provided by Totton J. Anderson (item 5), who conjures away all uncertainties[4]— until you turn to the next author. If item 6 (torn out of context for the good of the teaching cause) had not had a subject and you had had to provide one, following suit from items 1 through 5, what would you have used? Here what seems to be the same type of activity has another name, "lobbying"; an American authority, Edgar Lane, wrote the sentence,[5] from which it would seem reasonable to expect that the "men" who do the lobbying constitute a lobby. But James Bryce, for some years British ambassador in Washington, defined a lobby far more narrowly, restricting lobbying (item 7) to one sort of government decision, namely a legislative act.[6]

To the student and general reader, it is all very muddling; yet the muddle has been deliberately restricted. And if I were cruel enough to parade the fringe terms such as "organized group" (once favored in Britain by W. J. M. Mackenzie and Allen Potter), "private organization" (Bertram M. Gross), and "catalytic group" (Fred W. Riggs), you might well be inclined to throw up your hands in despair and opt for some simple subject such as astronomical physics in which (one likes to think) a name always "matches" an activity or observation.

Assuming you refuse to quit, how shall we proceed? We could hitch on to one of the scholars quoted and let ourselves be pulled clear of the morass. That would be the easiest way out for tutor or instructor, but not, in the long run, best for the student. Even if you are not going to specialize in political science, and even if your future career lies far from the college campus, you have to learn to fend for yourself in being able to cope independently with problems of definition, and with the underlying problems—the choice and formation of concepts. Certainly aspiring specialists must learn to be self-reliant in this special sense if they are to avoid becoming mere "scissors-and-paste" researchers. Besides, the state of the subdiscipline forming the focus for this volume warrants an attempt to rework some of the traditional material.

KINDS OF DEFINITION

The first step is to recognize what the authors cited above were offering their readers. Few of them thought it necessary to be explicit, but on the face of it

[1] S. E. Finer, in *Interest Groups on Four Continents*, ed. Henry W. Ehrmann (Pittsburgh: University of Pittsburgh Press, 1958), p. 237; N. C. Hunt, "Pressure Groups in the U.S.A.," *Occidente*, Vol. XII (1956), p. 114.

[2] *The Governmental Process* (New York: Alfred A. Knopf, Inc., 1951), p. 37.

[3] *Les Syndicats en France* (Paris: Armand Colin, 1963), p. 15. My translation.

[4] "Pressure Groups and Intergovernmental Relations," *The Annals*, Vol. 359 (May, 1965), p. 120, n. 6.

[5] *Lobbying and the Law* (Berkeley: University of California Press, 1964), pp. 8–9.

[6] *Modern Democracies*, Vol. II (London: Macmillan & Co. Ltd., 1929), p. 529. First published 1921.

most if not all were offering *nominal definitions*. The implied contrast is with what for centuries was called *real definition*:

> . . . two sorts into which definitions may be divided, *viz.* definition of names, and definition of things. The former are intended to explain the meaning of a term; the latter, the nature of a thing. . . .

That was written by John Stuart Mill,[7] who was about to attack the distinction, wishing to retain "definition" for use in relation only to names. Such a restriction is usual today: it is embodied, for instance, in the American philosopher Max Black's aphorism that definition "is more like a handshake than a sneeze: it is a social transaction." What he has in mind is that definition "is a process in which the use of a word (or other sign) is explained *by somebody* and *for somebody*."[8] Were we to follow Black, we could drop "nominal" and say that the authors quoted above were offering definitions. Even so we would not be out of the woods. For both *definition* in Black's sense and *nominal definition* are of two kinds, variously called:

lexical—stipulative (Robinson)

reported—stipulated (Black)

descriptive—stipulative (Hempel)[9]

A *lexical definition* embodies the reported usage of a word, usually as set out in some dictionary by a lexicographer. As a record of usage, it is supposed to have truth-value;[10] if it does, then insofar as our seven definitions are lexical, what we are landed with is a many-sided truth. On the other hand, a writer may say "Anyhow, that is how I mean the term"[11] and look around (one always feels) defiantly. To make such a declaration or proposal is to stipulate—hence *stipulative definition*. This has no truth-value and is, in some degree, arbitrary.[12]

---

[7] *A System of Logic*, 8th ed (London: Longmans, Green & Company Ltd., 1941), p. 92.

[8] *Critical Thinking* (New York: Prentice-Hall, Inc., 1946), p. 188.

[9] Richard Robinson, *Definition* (Oxford: Clarendon Press, 1950), pp. 18–19; Black, *ibid.*, p. 190; Carl Hempel, *Philosophy of Natural Science* (Englewood Cliffs, N. J.: Prentice-Hall, Inc., 1966), pp. 85–86.

[10] Robinson, *ibid.*, pp. 39 and 62–66.

[11] Harry Eckstein, *Pressure Group Politics* (London: George Allen & Unwin Ltd., 1960), p. 11.

[12] I use the qualifying phrase in order not to hold up the exposition. But I think Robinson is right on arbitrariness, and Giovanni Sartori's criticism misconceived. Robinson wrote (*Definition*, pp. 65–66): "In stipulation we freely make any word mean anything we choose, whereas in lexical definition we try to report truly what actual persons have actually meant by the word." Sartori argued (*Democratic Theory*, paperback ed. [New York: Frederick A. Praeger, Inc., 1965], p. 213): ". . . this is a distorted report of the actual proceedings. Actually innovation is very rare and certainly not our main concern. What we usually do is to make a choice among the existing meanings of a word. That is to say, our chief purpose is to reduce ambiguity." But Robinson was well aware of that, having already written (p. 60): "Often it consists merely in adopting one of the many common meanings of a common word and discarding the rest, that is, in announcing which of the established meanings you are going to use. The essence is that stipulative definition is the adoption of elementary sign-uses, while lexical definition is the reporting of them." That is "the strict sense in which stipulation is arbitrary and lexical definition is not" (p. 66). But they are both arbitrary "in the loose sense" that the connection between the word and the thing is conventional, contrived, man-made. No doubt, as Sartori properly insists (p. 211), today's lexical definitions are yesterday's stipulations, but equally we are not bound to accept these, but are free to innovate; and, in the social sciences, we perhaps do so more frequently than Sartori allows.

Accordingly, insofar as the seven definitions are stipulative, they are, in some degree, arbitrary, as indeed the inconsistencies between them suggest.

Of course, the authorities cited had their own purposes, and they could afford to forgo extended preliminaries because they were already familiar with the *thing* itself and already sensitized to some of the significant relationships included in it. You could ride on their coattails, but you would do better in the long run to "work through" to a definition instead. For, apart from the reasons already suggested, "working through" means trying out, as an expository device, some of the procedures traditionally known as *real definition*, and these encourage you to observe the world of everyday events in ways that assist or reinforce your understanding of the methods of political science.

Of the various types of real definition, the search for essences has probably been the most important historically. In this tradition, when we have discovered the essence of a thing (in the wide sense of *thing*), we have defined it. Here, evidently, we are not struggling or coping with a mere word or symbol, but with some real entity enjoying an objective existence "out there," beneath or beyond the surface phenomena. For our purpose, however, three types of (so-called) real definition are germane: abstraction, analysis, and synthesis.

Abstraction. This is the process of abstracting a universal (or general "form") from particulars. For example: in 1942 "many persons became aware for the first time of physiological shock, by studying the U.S. manual of first aid."[13] They suddenly recognized this thing in others or in themselves, but without having put a special name to it. They were thus able to identify the "form," SHOCK, which they labeled "shock." The sequence might be reconstructed as follows:

1. We observe a number of separate actions (or behaviors) by various people, in which—
2. We become aware of some common features (= a "form"), thus getting a pattern (or picture) in the head, so far unnamed, and
3. We name it.

Some authorities, e.g., J. Cook Wilson, a former professor of logic at Oxford, have counted this as a kind of real definition—"definition by abstraction."

Analysis. This dovetails into "definition by abstraction." Assume that we have gone through the process outlined just above. The product of that process —the pattern formed—may still be rather blurred in our minds. If it is, we shall have to embark upon getting the picture more in focus, upon replacing a clear idea with a distinct idea, as Leibniz put it. A pattern is clear if we can recognize instances of it; it is distinct (or vivid) if we can make a list of the features that distinguish this pattern from that one. For instance: we have identified that pattern of behavior, SHOCK, and named it "shock." But just what happens in the series of actions (or behaviors) thus singled out for special

[13] Robinson, *Definition*, p. 170.

attention as forming, in some loose sense, a unity?[14] Separating the parts from the whole, we probe and discriminate.

Synthesis. Whereas analysis discloses the complexities of a general "form," synthesis reveals that that "form" is itself a "unit" of some more all-embracing institution. In analysis, we work "downward" from an entity to its constituent parts; in synthesis, we move "upward" to a higher level where that entity (the "form" abstracted as in the section "Abstraction," above) can be seen as one component of a more complex whole. Having abstracted a *legislature*, for example, from the whole flow of political activity in a given period, we can analyze it into its component parts (government, opposition, official committees, party committees, etc.), but we can also synthesize it as one component of a constitution, or of a political system. This, too, has been thought of as a kind of real definition.

To sum up: Some senses in which *real definition* has been understood are:

1. Abstraction: The cognitive grasping of a *form*
2. Analysis (*going down*): Revealing the complexity of a *form*
3. Synthesis (*going up*): Revealing that a certain *form* is itself part of a still more complex whole[15]

In each case, the point is not to manipulate *words* but to discover the nature of *things*.

Let us go in search of *interest group*, using these three types of real definition as our guides.

[14] *Ibid.*, p. 172.
[15] *Ibid.*, p. 190.

ABSTRACTION AND NAMING

ABSTRACTION

In principle, then, we sweep the board clean of nominal definitions and set off in pursuit of the *real thing* that constitutes the subject of this volume. The *words* that we ignore for the present we shall return to later. For now let us take abstraction as our guide. But before we do, we should be clear that abstraction always entails an attribution of *meaning* by the Abstracter or Observer. For the "same" physical or bodily movements may have quite different social meanings. Imagine (to adapt freely from British anthropologist Raymond Firth[1]) you are out in the jungle. Suddenly fifty natives come crashing out of the undergrowth and advance upon you, clenched fists in the air. Are they expressing class solidarity with the workers of the world or—as you fear—do they merely intend to eat you? You discover that they are welcoming you, and you are glad, after all, that you came. On the face of it: the same behaviors, or activities (shaking of clenched fist), but three (at least) different social meanings. Again, a man is seen putting a cross on a piece of paper: what does that raw behavior mean? Is he (a) just doodling, (b) playing ticktacktoe (noughts and crosses), (c) ending a letter to his girlfriend, or (d) voting (where there are no voting machines) for his favorite, or least disliked, political party? So we conclude: the very same bodily movements or gestures can have utterly different social meanings. Conversely, different bodily movements or gestures (= "acts") may have the same social meaning. We might say, perhaps, that clenched fist = smile = (social meaning of) welcome.

So Observer's very first and inescapable job is to attribute *meaning* to what he observes, which comes down, crudely, to a judgment of purpose *in* what

[1] *Elements of Social Organization* (London: C. A. Watts and Co. Ltd., 1961), p. 23. Read pp. 22–27.

6

is being done. This, then, is the first step in abstraction, easy to overlook because we take it almost automatically and, within a common culture, quite accurately. Note well that from the very beginning of his interpretation Observer goes beyond what one school in political (and social) science would have considered to be "the hard facts."[2] Abstraction does not live by *observables* alone, but in principle gives full weight to *inferables* or *dispositionals*,[3] such as motives and attitudes. But how can Observer be certain that his inferences are correct, either at this stage or generally? How, at the outset, can Observer be certain that he shares the *act-meaning* of the Actor? He cannot be certain of it, but there are grounds for thinking it probable. These are general and specific. The first turns on what the Cambridge mathematician E. W. Hobson called "a body of common knowledge of the perceptual world,"[4] the base for what we might call "a body of common knowledge of the conceptual world." The specific grounds are twofold. In particular situations, Observer may be able to rely on *contextualization* (as Raymond Firth put it). One knows from the context whether the observed act of marking a cross on paper = doodling, symbolic kissing, voting, etc. Alternatively, or in addition, one can *ask* Actors what their acts mean to them.[5]

It is also vital to grasp that this attribution of meaning to raw behavior is only the first stage in abstraction, which has two steps, not one. Having infused raw behavior with meaning, Observer is unlikely to stop there; he has an inquiring mind and will want to be able to explain what it all means in a wider sense, "it" being the instantaneously decoded behavior, not the raw behavior. This is the second step: meaning to the Observer in terms of some frame of reference, some systematic body of knowledge, or at least some prior knowledge and trained judgment. For instance, to the Observer as political scientist, the sequence might be that shown in Figure 1. Here the political scientist, correctly

---

[2] If we accept this *meanings* approach, it is hard to see how we can avoid coming down in favor of one of the two great approaches in social (including political) science, the one that stresses (at this stage) its difference from, as against its similarity to, the natural sciences (or some of these, notably physics). As expressed by philosopher Alfred Schutz: ". . . the observational field of the social scientist—social reality—has a specific meaning and relevance structure for the human beings living, acting and thinking within it." Whereas ". . . the world of nature, as explored by the natural scientist, does not 'mean' anything to molecules, atoms and electrons" (in *Philosophy of the Social Sciences*, ed. Maurice Natanson [New York: Random House, Inc., 1963], p. 242). This seems so obviously true that one wonders why anybody bothers to dispute it, but disputed it is. On the other hand, it represents, I believe, the wave of the future. The Behavioralist movement of the late 1960's, e.g., contrary to much British and especially Oxonian opinion, is prepared to truck with *meaning*. But note well that the acceptance of the *meanings* approach is by no means ruinous of political *science*. Schutz himself acknowledged that. Mulford Sibley, in his judicious summing-up (*The Limits of Behavioralism in Political Science*, ed. James C. Charlesworth [Philadelphia: American Academy of Political and Social Science, 1962], p. 79), is surely right to say: ". . . the fact that common meanings must be identified before behavioral studies can proceed does not mean that the procedure of verification and empirical validation cannot take place by methods not unlike those utilized in the natural sciences."

[3] Richard S. Rudner, *Philosophy of Social Science* (Englewood Cliffs, N.J.: Prentice-Hall, Inc., 1966), pp. 21–23.

[4] *The Domain of Natural Science* (Cambridge, Eng.: Cambridge University Press, 1923), pp. 23–25.

[5] On the whole question, see Abraham Kaplan, *The Conduct of Inquiry* (San Francisco: Chandler Publishing Co., 1964).

Figure 1

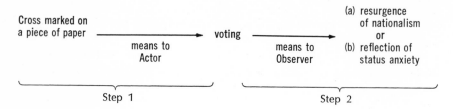

or not, explains the votes cast for a political party in terms of resurgent national-ism, or the votes cast for the wing of a party (e.g., the Radical Right in the United States) in terms of status anxiety, and so on. Clearly, the Actors (= voters) have now been left far behind; the Observer has the stage, and is trying to put their instantaneously decoded behavior into some explanatory framework.

To sum up in the language of Abraham Kaplan,[6] what one first observes is an *act* (= raw behavior). To the act an Observer attributes an act-meaning for the Actor, which yields an *action* (= instantaneously decoded behavior). Actions constitute the "units" or referents of political science. When the Observer sets out to inquire what the *actions* amount to, or mean, in some wider framework, and how the *actions* are related to other *actions* and situations, he is initiating a distinctive mode of interpretation, scientific, as against the first mode, semantic. The distinctions are charted in Figure 2.

Abstraction as a Kind of Real Definition. Let us now press these distinctions into service, undertaking a stage-one abstraction (Kaplan's semantic interpreta-tion) that will eventually lead us to one kind of (so-called) real definition of *interest group*. (A stage-two abstraction—Kaplan's scientific interpretation—is attempted partly in the section on synthesis, where interest groups are placed in the framework of a type of social system, but above all in Chapter Four, where the determinants of the styles of action of interest groups are elucidated.) For stage one we have to try out a kind of "mental experiment" (as the German sociologist Max Weber called it) because the relevant intellectual history (i.e., of the general "forms" that concern us) has yet to be written.

[6] *Ibid.*

Figure 2

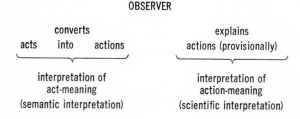

Think back to Albany, the New York State Capital, in the 1820's and 1830's,[7] when one of the relevant "forms" was crystallizing. Then reconstruct from Figure 3 (p. 10), reading from the bottom up.

Pause for a moment on a rung of the abstraction ladder[8] and survey the scene. You will notice:

(1) The extent to which the so-called "facts" (either in the primary sense of the raw behavior or *acts*, or, arguably, in the derivative sense of the *action*) have been selected from a limitless flow, on the basis, at its simplest, of curiosity.

(2) That the different acts are judged to have had the same act-meaning, and so qualify as the same action.

(3) That if, as presented, Observer's "decoding" appears slow, that is because we are seeing the past with the eyes of the present. There must have been a time when the context was "fluid" and the interpretation problematic. The conversation within the precincts *might* have been about an ordinary business deal or about the outcome of a horserace elsewhere in the state (or in New Orleans); the wining and dining, the marks of a generous soul. It would have taken further observation to give solid ground for the translation of the various *acts* into the *action*. Eventually, of course, the experienced Observer would be able to make immediate decodings of the raw behavior, from which others would learn, and so the notion would spread and take hold.

(4) That this decoding makes little sense unless we assume that the legislators would *not* have passed the bill without Actor's intervention. (This is crucial to the discussion of influence, or power.)

In any event, we reconstruct an *action*[9]:

Influencing legislators to pass (or modify, or reject) a bill

We are now well on the way. In due course, higher up the ladder, Observer could be expected to "generalize" the action, i.e., to extract a

[7] I reached these dates in this way. For the purposes of exposition, I made a start where the ancestors of the *word* "lobby" first gained currency, namely, in the United States. The "where" is easier than the exact "when." Karl Schriftgiesser (*The Lobbyists* [Boston: Little, Brown and Company, 1951], p. 3) gives "lobby-agent" 1829, but relies on H. L. Mencken, who himself cites no source (*The American Language* [New York: Alfred A. Knopf, Inc., 1919; 2nd ed., 1921], p. 98). Mencken records that "lobbyist" (a journalistic contraction, according to Schriftgiesser) followed quickly on the heels of "lobby-agent." If so, it seems not to have caught on at the time, but by 1847, when Chauncey Goodrich of Yale revised Webster (2nd ed., revised and enlarged), there was "lobby-member": "a person who frequents the lobby of a house of legislation," which by the 1860's his successor was making more explicit by adding ". . . for the purpose of influencing measures" (1864 ed., by Noah Porter). Or, as others had said of the same term: ". . . in order to influence the action of the members" (*Worcester's Dictionary*, 1860). As such terms as these are not to be found in the Websters of 1806 (*Compendious Dictionary*), the 1828–29 period, or 1847, or in the John Pickering of 1815 (*A Vocabulary or Collection of Words and Phrases which have been supposed to be peculiar to the United States* [Cambridge, Mass.]), we may hazard the guess that the ancestors of "lobby" ("lobby-agent" and especially "lobby-member") were coming into use but not yet common sometime in the 1820's and 1830's.

[8] For the origin of this concept, see S. I. Hayakawa, *Language in Thought and Action*, 2nd. ed. (London: George Allen & Unwin Ltd., 1965), Chap. 10; and Alfred Korzybski, *Science and Sanity*, 3rd. ed. (Lakeville, Conn.: International Non-Aristotelian Library Publishing Co., 1948).

[9] Neither here nor throughout should Kaplan be held responsible for my very free adaptation and illustration of his *acts* and *actions*. I believe, however, that I have kept to the spirit of his distinctions.

Figure 3

≡

ACTION   INFLUENCING LEGISLATORS TO PASS (OR MODIFY, OR REJECT) A BILL

≡

(Inexperienced Observer asks himself: What did that behavior mean to the banking representative? He reserves judgment but continues to observe, gather and weigh up evidence, possibly as follows:

1) He attends subsequent meetings and sessions of the legislature, and notes that a bill is quickly passed favoring the concern with which Actor, the banking representative, is associated.
2) He interviews Actor.
3) He samples the views of Legislators about the bill, including some of those he had seen with Actor.

Armed with this and other relevant information, and having the gift of empathy, he reconstructs the raw acts, turning these into an action, crystallized above.)

≡

ACTS
Within precincts, a man identifiable as a spokesman for banking interests is observed in the company of some legislators. Man speaks, the others nod, they shake hands, disperse.

That evening, whole group seen wining and dining at expensive out-of-town restaurant. Bankers' representative seen to pay the bill.

≡

Total flow of activity within
New York State Legislature

≡

TOTAL FLOW OF POLITICAL ACTIVITY IN USA
(in certain period)

≡

Read from here ——————————————▶

general "form" from his observations at Albany and from what he had seen or read about, say, the work of the U. S. Temperance Union (1833) vis-à-vis other state legislatures as well as other similar activities at Washington itself—for instance: (a) the pro-tariff efforts of the wool growers; of the Philadelphia Society for the Promotion of National Industry; of the Pennsylvania Society for the Encouragement of Manufactures and the Mechanic Arts; (b) the anti-slavery efforts of the American Anti-Slavery Society (1833). Reflecting on this and other experience, the Observer would have come to isolate the general "form," something along the lines of:

PRIVATE PERSON OR PERSONS (AS SPECIFIED) ATTEMPTING TO INFLUENCE LEGISLATORS

IN RESPECT OF LEGISLATION (AS SPECIFIED)

This will be referred to from now on as a concept, which in this book will always mean a nonlinguistic entity as distinct from a word. For we are still assuming that the procedure just adopted enables us to construct the concept as *if* the question of naming it had not yet arisen. More starkly, the concept could be represented by:

$$PP\ (a,\ b,\ \dots)\ \longrightarrow\ L:G\ (j,\ k,\ \dots)$$

where PP = Private Person(s), L = Legislators, and G = Goal (the legislative policy or decision sought).

Ideally, we should now scrutinize the evidence in many other countries, but let British experience do duty for the remainder. While lobby-agents or lobby-members were busy at Albany, private persons in Britain were brandishing petitions to Parliament as never before, the number of these in the five years ending in 1831 being twenty times that of the last five years of the previous century. Some were on a vast scale: the Anti-Slavery Petition of 1833 bore no fewer than a million and a half signatures. Evidently, this was a mode of popular agitation, exemplified also by the great petitions of 1831–32 for parliamentary reform,[10] which, on a far smaller scale, had been the subject of petitions from the 1780's.

The British experience (just hinted at here) can be assimilated to the American by way of the reconstruction shown in Figure 4 (again reading from the bottom up): Here, as before, an Observer may be deemed to be climbing the ladder of abstraction, separating out certain acts (appropriate to the old parliamentary procedure) and decoding these as actions.

Now one of these actions would "correspond" to the Anti-Slavery Petition of 1833. But an Observer would have also taken note of the Anti-Slavery Society's address to the nation published in the press in 1830. The Society urged electors at the forthcoming parliamentary election to let their:

> . . . first question to every candidate be, are you a Proprietor of Slaves, or a West India merchant? If the answer is in the affirmative, we would recommend to you a positive refusal, unless he be one of the very few

---

[10] Cecil S. Emden, *The People and the Constitution*, 2nd ed. (London: Oxford University Press, 1962), pp. 77–78.

Figure 4

ACTION   PETITIONING PARLIAMENT TO BRING ABOUT SPECIFIED RESULTS

ACTS { Crowd gathers outside House of Commons, talking and gesticulating. Some are carrying parchment, which they take and present to Members. Debate follows.

Total flow of activity within
precincts of Parliament

TOTAL FLOW OF POLITICAL ACTIVITY IN BRITAIN
(in certain period)

Read from here ──────────────►

who have already proved themselves true friends to our cause; or who, being known to you as a man of probity and honor, will give you the security of his promise henceforth to support it in the House. But whoever the candidate may be, demand of him, as the condition of your support, that he will solemnly pledge himself to attend in his place whenever any measure is brought forward for the termination of Slavery by parliamentary enactments; and that he will give his vote for every measure of that kind.[11]

Evidently, such activity bore the same *meaning* as the same Society's mass petition. Extend the observations generally and eventually you have a concept:

PRIVATE PERSON OR PERSONS (AS SPECIFIED) ATTEMPTING TO INFLUENCE PARLIAMENT

IN RESPECT OF LEGISLATION (AS SPECIFIED)

Or, in cut-down form;

$$PP\ (c, d, \ldots) \longrightarrow Parl. : G\ (l, m, \ldots)$$

[11] The Anti-Slavery Society's address to the nation, July 7, 1830 (*The Scotsman*, July 24, 1830), in A. Aspinall and E. Anthony Smith (eds.), *English Historical Documents*, XI (London: Eyre and Spottiswoode, 1959), p. 811. With the permission of Eyre and Spottiswoode (Publishers) Ltd., London, and Oxford University Press, Inc., New York.

Here, then, is another *thing* that we have isolated from the total flow of social interactions and in that sense defined. Alternatively expressed, observable behaviors of individual persons have been isolated, "sewn together," invested with meaning, and so converted into actions and then into concepts. Obviously this has nothing to do with defining a *word*: roughly, we have found some *thing* but not labeled it.

NAMING

What *shall* we call it, then? In principle, we are free to hang on any label: we just announce "This thing we have just discovered (= abstracted) is going to be known as. . . ." It would be fun to think up some striking label—my favorite is "syzygy"—but its use at this point in time would puzzle other political scientists (and annoy astronomers if they got to hear of it). In practice, as we all know, certain labels have been preempted. "Lobby-agent," "lobby-member," "lobbyer," and "lobbyist" (notice that intriguing emphasis on the "immediate" Actor rather than the acting), as well as the perhaps more generalized noun "lobby," were the labels produced by American observers well over a century ago in every case. Some of these labels, or signs, were adopted fairly quickly by the British (e.g., "lobbyer" in the 1870's; "lobbyist" and "lobby"—the noun still—in the 1890's), and not as museum pieces but to designate their own political practices. Some of the signs, of course, have fallen into disuse, but others, with the concomitant verbal forms, continue to flourish today, and in general they still virtually designate the things that they designated a century ago.

That being so, we may as well accept the signs actually in use. But it is essential to recognize what that acceptance entails, and what, for that matter, the prior diffusion of "lobbyist," "lobby," etc., from the United States to Britain entailed to begin with. The effect of both must be to raise the level of abstraction, which is always achieved at the cost of dropping some characteristics overboard like ballast from a balloon. Consequently, the diffusion necessarily entailed distortion from the first. It was exactly *as if* an Observer, striving to relate American to British experience, set out to "generalize" the two concepts already elucidated, thus (from the bottom up):

$$PA \longrightarrow L : G$$

$$PP\ (a, b, \ldots) \longrightarrow L : G\ (j, k, \ldots)\qquad PP\ (c, d, \ldots) \longrightarrow Parl : G\ (l, m, \ldots)$$

American case   **British case**

But the relevant situation in the two countries was never identical. For example: the *PP* (= Private Persons) now assimilated into *PA* (= Private Actors) were substantially different, there being already greater role specialization (= "professionalization") in the United States. Analysis will disclose further distortions; it is enough now to see that although the British took over the American-invented sign, they did not have the designated thing in its entirety. They could have paid tribute to the differences, while yet acknowledging the common elements, by writing Lobby^B (or Lobby$_2$), as against Lobby^{USA} (or Lobby$_1$). In fact, as perhaps is normal with diffusion, they took the symbol neat and let the differences "go hang," which was tantamount to moving up the ladder of abstraction to:

$$PA \longrightarrow L : G$$

Once the higher conceptual level has been reached (by historical "dialectic" or simply by armchair reflection), a further distinction may become necessary. Other types of Private Actor(s) may grow important outside the earlier context and so require verbal demarcation. This happened, of course, with the political parties, which were still undeveloped when lobbying first got under way. Partly for that reason, early usage in the United States did not make the distinction, although at times it was approached, as when, at about mid-century, lexicographers began to exclude "members of the legislature" from "a lobby." Once the parties as engines for gaining power, and hence for public policy-making, have become major institutions, the distinction needs to be made (imperfect though it is). Thus the stripped-down version of our concept has to become:

$$PA \text{ (not being Pol. P.)} \longrightarrow L : G$$

This (at last) is what, if one tradition were perpetuated and extended, we could call a real definition of LOBBY, to which the symbol "lobby," or a variant, could be (and historically was) attached.

What we seek, however, is a real definition of INTEREST GROUP. For this the way has now been prepared, and we can proceed more briskly. To the concept LOBBY we "add" this one:

$$PA \text{ (not being Pol. P.)} \longrightarrow E : G$$

where E = Executive (or Administration). This embraces those activities whose terminal point is constituted by such bodies as a French or British Cabinet, such a person (or office) as an American President, or by the civil servants. Arguably, the public corporations (as in Britain and France) ought to be included; it depends on where we draw the line between "public" and "private," which here is largely a matter of convenience. Either way, the abstraction of the general concept is certain, as usual, to entail the blanketing of many lower-level differences in the several situations.

As for the allocation of a sign to this concept, history does not help, except perhaps negatively in that our predecessors do not seem to have found it necessary to conjure up a name. It so happened that the Private Actor(s) that concern us obtruded themselves sufficiently to gain attention and naming at a time of legislative supremacy or at least predominance. Hence the terminal point of the activity could be conceived as *Legislators*. When, however, the balance began to tip in favor of (members of) Executives, which then attracted the ventured (or attempted) influence of Private Actors, it seems that this variant was given the old name. That is, the old sign was apparently "stretched" to cover the new (or in the British case, the revived) development. But as yet the evidence for a definitive view of the conceptual development has hardly begun to be collected.

Happily, that does not obstruct us. We need this concept simply as part of an upward classifying "thrust" or build-up;[12] the point is merely to reach our summit. In order to get there, we, the observing political scientists, do not, at this late stage, require a *name* for the concept. If we were in a fanciful mood, we could dub it "youyou" (that French word which looks as if it ought to be English). Otherwise we can just leave the "box" empty. Either way, the procedure is simply to "unite" the two concepts. The effect of this is to generalize the objects of ventured influence; L "plus" E yields *Pub. T.*, or Public Target (target = something to be affected by an action or development). Thus Figure 5, reading from the bottom up.

In this we reach our destination. This is the concept we have on our hands if we "follow through" consistently from raw behavior (or acts) to actions to concepts, taking care to "lift" consistently from one level of abstraction to another (as with *PP* to *PA*, *L* and *Parl.* to *L*, and *L* and *E* to *Pub. T.*), and to make certain exclusions as we go along. As such this either is, or ought (in my view) to become, *the* concept to whose isolation and analysis we are implicitly committed in this volume. It has its foundation in observed behaviors, interpretations, and conceptual distinctions established for over a century, although it is not confined to these in detail, since some of the steps in the "dialectic" seem to have been "missing" and have had to be supplied—(e.g., the concept *PA (not Pol. P.)* $\longrightarrow$ *E : G*). Despite that, it probably comes close to the concept that political scientists harbored at the end of the 1960's; if we still believed in essences, we could say that it captures the essence of the entity we are required to discuss.

The question of the naming of the concept, on the other hand, is more debatable. In principle, once again, we are free to choose any sign (or symbol), and in the long run political scientists probably ought to seek agreement upon one (they do not seem to have ever seriously tried by way of *real* definition). Meanwhile, there seem to be only five horses in the race and only three in the

---

[12] Compare: "While division breaks up a genus into species, classification is the grouping of individuals into classes, and these classes into wider ones." Morris R. Cohen and Ernest Nagel, *An Introduction to Logic and Scientific Method* (New York: Harcourt, Brace and Co., 1934), p. 241.

Figure 5

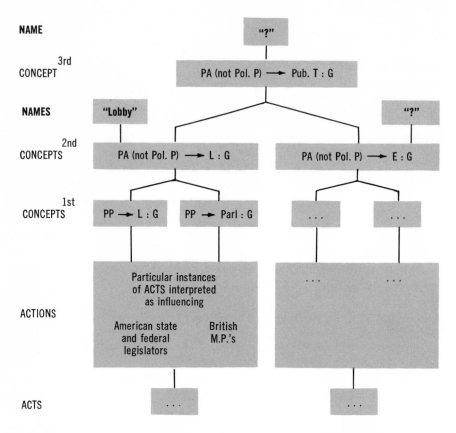

TOTAL FLOW OF POLITICAL ACTIVITY IN CERTAIN COUNTRIES
(in certain period)

Read from here ⟶

betting. The two outsiders are evidently "organized group" and "private organization." Even if these terms commanded more support than they have attracted, they would not be adopted here. Since "organized" does not distinguish between public and private groups, we would be driven to saying "organized private groups." There is, besides, a further objection: in the following chapter, where we attempt that kind of real definition which has been known as synthesis, the *PA* of our concept is depicted as a species of secondary group for which "organized group" and especially "private organization" are possible synonyms.

To dub the concept "lobby" would commend itself to such authorities as Samuel Finer (in his later work), and might suit Edgar Lane, Lester Milbrath (since his study of the Washington lobbyists disclosed that they are as much concerned with executive-branch as legislative-branch decisions),[13] and others. In terms of my scheme "lobby" *could* be made to cover the first two concepts isolated, the one symbolized by "lobby" and the other playfully indicated by "youyou." That being so, "lobby" would then stand for the higher-level concept also, since this incorporates the two lower-level concepts.

For various reasons, however, that course is not followed here. In the United States from Boston to Baton Rouge (to cite the north–south range of my own inquiries), "lobby" is as derogatory an epithet as one can think of; certainly no less so than "pressure group." Even if "lobby" smelt sweeter, the relationship of thing to sign that it embodies has been fairly consistently maintained for over a century—i.e., the terminal target has been thought of as constituted by *Legislators*. As a particular case of that usage, "lobbyist" has long had a special, even legal, meaning in the United States. All in all, the adoption of "lobby" (and its cognates) for our concept is hardly to be recommended.

"Pressure group" may be less perturbing if "pressure" is read as a useful metaphor recalling, as with Harry Eckstein, that argument itself is a kind of pressure. As for usage, "pressure" in exactly the relevant sense has been in circulation even in Britain since at least 1877. On the other hand, it must be admitted that the "feeling-tone" of the term is derogatory. Above all, the use of "pressure" tends to make us revert to thinking in terms of raw behavior, of mere acts as distinct from act-meanings. More loosely, by using "pressure" we tend to define the Actor in terms of the methods he employs. A Private Actor makes use of a variety of procedures (acts), only some of which could reasonably be designated "pressure," but the meaning of those procedures (acts) *to* the Actor is the same. By contrast, "pressure group" tends to direct attention to some methods to the neglect of others, at the same time destroying the unity of *act-meaning* and name.

Would we fare any better with "interest group"? It seems little less derogatory than "pressure group": if pressure is to be deplored, interests are suspect, commonly attracting the adjectives "sinister," "vested," or "special." On the other hand, in recent years a strong tide has been running for this usage, even engulfing David Truman's "political interest group." Fashions may have to be resisted, but as it happens the usage goes back further than most political scientists realize. In 1929, an anonymous reviewer of those studies of the day that are now clearly landmarks (*Pressure Politics* and *Group Representation before Congress*) wrote:

> The first mentioned of these two books consists of an intensive study of the activities of two interest groups, namely the Anti-Saloon League and the United States Brewers' Association. The latter book presents a survey of many of the interest groups having headquarters in Washington.[14]

Even that is not conclusive; it merely means that the recent tendency to use "interest group" is a resurgence of the tide, and that the tradition is older

---

[13] See beginning of Chapter One. Finer's definition there dates from September, 1957. When he came to write one of the two pioneering books in the British literature (*Anonymous Empire*, [London: Pall Mall Press Ltd., 1958]), he plumped for "lobby." Milbrath's book is *The Washington Lobbyists* (Chicago: Rand McNally & Co., 1963).

[14] *The Annals*, Vol. 144 (July, 1929), p. 160.

than is commonly thought if perhaps unable to boast of continuity. Our choice of labels is circumscribed by tradition but not determined by it. However, except possibly for Alfred de Grazia's "political group," which curiously has never had many admirers, nothing better seems to be at hand. Accordingly, as something less than ardent suitors, we address ourselves to "interest group." But we must be crystal clear that this is a technical term exactly on a par with "syzygy" and "youyou" (or "x"). Its selection is logically independent of the inherited usage of either "interest" or "group," which means that we do not have to lie awake at night wondering how far these terms "match" the concept we have constructed, how far groups have interests, what these interests consist in—all of which would surely prompt us to ask: "Well, what *is* an interest?" Samuel Krislov, for example, asked that question in taking Harry Eckstein to task for a "cursory" treatment of the notion of interests.[15] But for our purpose in this volume at least, that is exactly the kind of question we have tried to avoid. The scientific procedure is to observe and isolate certain acts (or behaviors) and actions, and to collect these into "bundles" whose interconnections may prove fruitful. "Interest group" being just a convenient label for one such "bundle," it need have no connection at all with the meaning of its two constituent terms. Historically, the connections are obvious, but these constitute an "extra," an uncovenanted benefit; the parts should not be thought of separately but collectively, for the term is indivisible. Precisely for that reason it should always (I believe) be hyphenated: "interest-group."

The adoption of "interest-group," even without the hyphen, has very important implications for the rest of the names in stock. If the concept LOBBY is to be incorporated in the higher-level concept INTEREST-GROUP, the noun "lobby" ought in general to be superannuated in favor of "interest-group." Its retention could be justified only if there were complete specialization of function: that is, if a *PA* confined his ventured influence to Legislators only. If a *PA* has other public targets, such as (the members of) Executives, then his activities are conceptualized at the higher level where *L* joins *E*. Similarly, had there been a specialized term for ventured influence upon the Executive (other than my "youyou"), it too would disappear as a noun, becoming symbolized at the higher level, unless Observer found complete specialization of function. Does such complete specialization of function exist? It does not appear so. Even the American lobbyist now sets out to influence the executive, or administration, although for legal reasons to do with the federal and state regulation of lobbying, the term may at present have to be retained in the United States. But, in general, where there are no such complications, political scientists today need only "interest-group."

What this in turn means is that an interest-group today is typically *a bit of* a lobby, and *a bit of* a youyou (or whatever). These are roles that an interest-group combines in varying proportions (over time, too), so that, ultimately, what we as political scientists need is not simply a classificatory, or categorial, concept (as here laboriously built up), but a variable concept, indicating the degree to which an interest-group *lobbies*, and the degree to which it undertakes other activities

[15] "What Is an Interest?" *Western Political Quarterly*, Vol. XVI (December, 1963), p. 830.

of the relevant kind. In fact, while we could now dispense with the inherited nouns, we require more verbs. It has already been pointed out that the classification implied in the early nineteenth-century terminology turned upon the nature or identity of the Actor(s): "lobby-agent," "lobby-member," "lobby," and "lobbyist" had the field first. That focus was (in effect) maintained by the introduction of "pressure group" and "interest group." Such formulations were presumably necessary, but in time they tended to make prisoners of many political scientists, who, long after the situation had changed, still conceived of diverse (types of) Private Actors rather than of a single (type of) Private Actor doing diverse things. Today, however, it is increasingly recognized that interest-groups generally undertake in *some* degree the activities originally covered by the noun "lobby," by whatever ought to have been used instead of "youyou," and by "pressure group."

And so we need verbs: for the activities of interest-groups vis-à-vis (a) Legislators and (b) members of Executives, including in both instances whatever is deemed to have been indicated by "pressure group." For (a), "to lobby" is the obvious candidate and had better be accepted. In order, as observing political scientists, to make the distinction between face-to-face and other comparatively direct approaches on the one hand, and more oblique approaches on the other (e.g., public relations campaigns), we might follow one of two courses:

(1) We might rely upon adverbs: to lobby *directly* (meaning the absence of any intervening agency or instrumentality) or *indirectly* (some agency or instrumentality intervening, possibly making more than one "step"). Correspondingly we would have the gerunds, or verb-nouns, "direct lobbying" and "indirect lobbying."

(2) Alternatively, we might reserve "to lobby" for the direct approaches and produce another word for the indirect. A possible candidate might be "to propagandize." This, however, has disquieting overtones, although we might stress the original sense of *winning adherents*, and not necessarily by public campaigns.

As for (b), the solution is not obvious: no special words seem ever to have been conjured up. Until political scientists as a profession reach a working agreement, the procedure may have to be that outlined as number 1 above, specifying the Target. Happily, we do not have to propound a solution here: it is enough, *en passant*, to recognize the problem and to go forward grasping the concept of a (single type of) Private Actor undertaking a variety of actions previously encapsulated in words indicating a variety of (types of) Private Actors.

CHAPTER THREE

ANALYSIS, SYNTHESIS, CLASSIFICATION

ANALYSIS

We saw in Chapter One that analysis has been considered by some authorities to be a form of real definition. We may begin our consideration of it by working with the cut-down representation of the concept which last appeared (p. 16) as:

PA (not Pol. P.) ⟶ Pub. T. : G

(= Private Actor, other than Political Party, ventures influence upon Public Target in order to secure some Goal). Examine first the qualification *not Pol. P.* The stock distinction between groups that seek political office and groups that seek only to influence those in office is by no means discriminating enough for every context. In the first place, since some interest-groups develop into parties, there must be a point in time when the identification is uncertain. Take this example from British experience:

Stage 1	1890's	trade unions
		Fabian Society
		Social Democratic Federation (SDF)
		Independent Labour Party (ILP)
Stage 2	1900	Labour Representation Committee (LRC) formed from the four groups above—2 members elected to Parliament
Stage 3	1903	LRC group in Parliament (now 5) required by conference resolution to "have done with Liberalism and Toryism and every other 'ism' that is not Labourism."
Stage 4	1906	LRC group in Parliament (now 29) decides to call itself "the Labour party."

The unions and the Fabian Society, if not the SDF and the ILP, would count as interest-groups. The four entities came together in 1900 as the LRC. But it was not until 1903 that the LRC group in Parliament was required (by conference resolution) to form "a distinct group" and "to abstain strictly from identifying themselves with or promoting the interests of any section of the Liberal or Conservative parties," and the name "party" did not follow until 1906. It would be a bold man who would undertake to fit the interest-group concept to each of these stages.

In France the Poujadist Union de Défense des Commerçants et des Artisans (UCDA) would have to be ranked initially (say, 1953–55) as an interest-group. By 1956, however, with 53 members in the new National Assembly, it had acquired the look if not the name (Union et Fraternité Française, UFF) of a party.[1] Its flame soon spluttered and went out (1957–58), but the contrast with the Labour party in Britain is not simply this virtual extinction but the failure to exhibit that constitutionalist ethos without which a group is less a party, *as usually understood*, than a movement or even a conspiracy. So, after the 1956 election, what *was* Poujadism in terms of our concept here?

What are we to make, also, of the many tiny parties that go through the motions of competing in American presidential elections? Are these not less parties than interest-groups? Recall, too, the interesting life-cycle of the Liberal party in Britain, not unlike that of families in the Lancashire aphorism "clogs to clogs in three generations." That is, in the 1870's several reform interest-groups self-consciously fused as the National Liberal Federation,[2] later to be identified with the Liberal party, which had a period of glory but today enjoys goodwill but no prospects at all of forming a government. So, arguably, the sequence could be rendered as:

Interest-group ⟶ political party ⟶ interest-group

Or consider a very different party in the German Federal Republic in the late 1950's: the BHE (Bund der Heimatvertriebenen und Entrechteten),[3] whose core was made up of refugees from the lost territory beyond the Oder–Neisse line. During the 1957 election campaign it had to meet "the charge of being nothing but an interest group," and accordingly adopted some broader policies "which it hoped would make it more of a party and less of a pressure group."[4]

Such instances as these serve to illustrate that the line of demarcation between interest-group and political party is not invariably easy to discern, but this hardly constitutes a serious obstacle to effective observation and discussion. More serious are the instances where relative clarity of line has been, in effect, obscured by the nature of the working relationship between interest-groups and parties. In his celebrated study of the Anti-Saloon League (responsible for the

---

[1] Philip M. Williams, *Crisis and Compromise*, 3rd ed. of *Politics in Post-War France* (London: Longmans, Green & Company Ltd., 1964), pp. 162–66.
[2] Samuel H. Beer, *British Politics in the Collectivist Age* (New York: Alfred A. Knopf, Inc., 1965), p. 53, citing the British political scientist Hugh Berrington.
[3] Association of the Homeless and Those Deprived of Their Rights.
[4] U. W. Kitzinger, *German Electoral Politics* (Oxford: Clarendon Press, 1960), pp. 176–80.

18th Amendment that made the United States officially "dry"), Peter Odegard traced its use of what he represented as the classic pressure-group (*read* interest-group) method—working through the existing party organizations.[5] As if in response to that but really as part of a general discussion, the Swedish political scientist Gunnar Heckscher remarked, almost thirty years later, that the American assumption that a pressure group is an extra-parliamentary body "working through different political parties" is apt to cause confusion in Western Europe, where some groups, for example, are "affiliated to specific party organizations."[6] For us the significance of that remark is twofold. On the one hand, in some political systems the claims of the major groups (in a diffuse sense) are usually projected *by* the interest organizations *through* particular parties: thus, in Sweden itself, the claims of the manual workers are articulated by the Federation of Labor and projected through the Social-Democratic party.[7] Similarly, farmers eventually reach up to the Center party; the white-collar workers, to both Liberals and Conservatives, and so on. So close (in the late Sixties) was the "intellectual" link between interest organizations and parties (and, presumably, so little the "autonomous," creative thinking by the parties as such) that if the organizations did not produce policies, the parties were left with little sense of direction.[8] The Italian situation of the late Fifties, on the other hand, is arresting for a related but different reason. It is not simply (sustaining Heckscher's point) that one of the union "peaks" (national confederations), the Confederazione Generale Italiana del Lavoro, worked through two parties, the Partito Comunista Italiano (PCI) and the Partito Socialista Italiano (PSI), or even that these three bodies were run by interlocking directorates, although that alone threatens the interest-group concept. It is also that the flow of policy was not in one direction only but traveled *from* party *to* interest-group as well. Nor did that hold good only on the Left. Another union "peak," the Confederazione Italiana Sindacati Lavoratori (CISL), was able to make its influence felt on the Democrazia Cristiana party (DC) "at several points on several issues."[9] On the other hand, through the good offices of a senator and some deputies, the DC "bounced back" on the CISL, which indeed was expected to follow party directives. How does that leave the interest-group concept? *Somewhat damaged,* which is the conclusion already reached on more fundamental grounds by the American political scientist Joseph LaPalombara, on whose work we have just been drawing.[10] It has indeed to be not so much shamefacedly admitted as openly proclaimed that empirical complexity does tend to undermine the universal application of the *PA (not Pol. P)* section of the concept. Full under-

[5] *Pressure Politics: The Story of the Anti-Saloon League* (New York: Columbia University Press, 1928), p. 80.

[6] *The Study of Comparative Government and Politics* (London: George Allen & Unwin Ltd., 1957), pp. 44–45.

[7] Björn Molin, "Swedish Party Politics: A Case Study," in *Scandinavian Political Studies,* Vol. 1 (Helsinki: Academic Bookstore, and New York: Columbia University Press, 1966), pp. 45–58.

[8] *Ibid.,* p. 51. But this is partly my reading of Professor Molin.

[9] Joseph LaPalombara, *The Italian Labor Movement: Problems and Prospects* (Ithaca, N.Y.: Cornell University Press, 1957), pp. 82–91.

[10] "The Utility and Limitations of Interest Group Theory in Non-American Field Situations," *Journal of Politics,* Vol. 22 (1960), pp. 29–49, for which a handy source is *Comparative Politics,* ed. Harry Eckstein and David A. Apter (New York: The Free Press, 1966), Part VI.

standing of that must attend upon our attempt at synthesis; it is sufficient now to say that politico-sociological concepts have the qualities (and so the limitations) of the material (the relevant social reality) from which they were constructed. Nevertheless, we do not have to throw our hand in; the distinction between interest-group and party remains a useful working one, which we can treat either as a first approximation, or as a "pure" standard of reference by which the relevant activity in specific political systems can be crudely "placed."

Having got so far, we will not continue to repeat the qualification *not Pol. P.* although it will always, *mutatis mutandis,* be implied. Ceasing to be so explicit in that respect focuses still more attention upon the "unburdened" *PA.* Take the first "term," *P.* That the *A* (= Actor) is private may seem too platitudinous to mention again, but it may not hold for every social system.[11] The question comes up for discussion later; meanwhile, we ought to be aware that the *P* carries overtones. As for the *A,* historically it has glossed over three distinctions, two of which are important. The unimportant one is that the *A* has never distinguished between an individual role and a collective role.[12] There is no reason to exclude from *A* the lone wolf, but he constitutes the limiting case. What the English philosopher Dorothy Emmet said of politics as a whole applies to this phase of it as well: politics as an activity "is something which one cannot do by oneself. It is a game of partners and opponents."[13] Accordingly, Actor is not usually given to playing a *principal role* (= acting in his own right) but a *representative role* (speaking for a social group).

The *A* of the concept, however, has never consistently distinguished between different types of *representative role.* Even at Albany, the early practitioners were not always specialists or professionals; at times, for example, a committee would descend upon the State Capitol. By the 1870's the lobby in the United States generally could be conceived of as an "outside pressure" by agents *and* principals.[14] The *A,* in short, glosses over the differences between a *spokesman role* and a *broker role.* It is a difference, in part, between unpaid and paid intermediaries, but not entirely so, since a spokesman role might be and is played by full-time association officials. At bottom the difference turns on the extent to which the *representative role* has undergone still further specialization, as with the (in principle) free-lancing, free-ranging lobbyists of the United States. Similar tendencies can be discerned in some other systems, but in varying degrees, so that the ratio of *spokesman role* to *broker role* also varies from system to system. All this is "hidden" in the *A;* but that, of course, is the price we have to pay for being high enough on the ladder of abstraction to be able to survey, if not the world, then some substantial portion of it. In a sense,

[11] *The Politics of the Developing Areas,* ed. Gabriel A. Almond and James S. Coleman, with Lucian Pye, Myron Weiner, Dankwart A. Rustow, and George I. Blanksten (Princeton, N. J.: Princeton University Press, 1960), p. 33. See below, p. 99.

[12] See above, p. 13.

[13] *Function, Purpose and Powers* (London: Macmillan & Co. Ltd., 1958), p. 113. Do not confuse all this with the methodological question about the empirical unit of observation, which is always an individual and his acts, there being no social group *as such* to observe. To look for a social group *as such* is to be guilty of reification, i.e., of making an abstraction concrete. Social groups are real (e.g., in influencing the behavior of their members), but they are not real in the same sense as an individual is real.

[14] John Russell Bartlett, *Dictionary of Americanisms,* 4th ed. (New York: Bartlett and Welford, 1877), under *lobby.*

however, we *can* eat our cake and have it *if* we learn to be sensitive to the ambiguities of the *A* in *PA*.

There is another ambiguity: *for whom* (= for what sort of social entity) is *A* spokesman or broker? There is nothing in the concept, as it emerges and develops, to distinguish between social groups *of* (bankers, wool merchants, manufacturers, trade unions) and social groups *for* (the ending of the slave trade and of slavery; Catholic Emancipation [*in* Britain, *from* political disabilities]; Temperance or Prohibition; woman suffrage). Such a distinction has been attempted by many writers, and *prima facie* it has some importance, but it can be sustained only by clambering so far down the ladder of abstraction that we can deal with no more than one or two political systems. If we seek some broader comparisons, we simply have to climb the ladder, discarding some detail in order to gain height.

Turn now to the other "end" of the concept. In accordance with the meaning that we Observers ascribe to the Actor's acts, we realize that here the Target (= something to be affected by an action or development) is always a Terminal Target, i.e., the institution where the required decision is actually taken. But students easily confuse a Terminal Target with an Intermediate Target, one struck by an interest-group for instrumental purposes only, i.e., to communicate influence to a Terminal Target. Thus most of the interest-group activity in the British Parliament is not intended to induce decisions by parliamentarians as such but by the Cabinet or government. Of course these "circles" overlap, but one circle actually decides, although by no means in splendid isolation from the others (not forgetting the very important party committees *in* if not *of* Parliament), which is why these "others" can be profitably used as Intermediate Targets. Notice here again the somewhat blurred view we get when high up on the ladder of abstraction. Not only do some political systems (Australia, the United States) have available many more Terminal Targets than others but their identity varies from one issue to another.

We now ask: Must a (Terminal) Target be Public? It is not uncommon to read of interest-groups within such private bodies as the World Council of Churches or the Confederation of British Industry (e.g., the Industrial Policy Group, an informal committee of major industrialists, formed in 1967). The net might also be said to catch the "parties" discovered within some American and British trade unions and British retail cooperatives.[15] The answer is that there is no *must* about it, i.e., no "essentialist"[16] reason for the restriction implied in *Pub. T.* It is simply a question of demarcating a convenient area of study. If we wished, we could extend the concept to include Private Targets. But ventured influence upon public bodies constitutes an important topic, and its investigation is quite enough to be going on with. No doubt the study of private government should be pursued, and ultimately the lines should converge if only because the internal processes of private groups must be factors in their ventured

[15] Seymour Martin Lipset, Martin A. Trow, and James S. Coleman, *Union Democracy* (Glencoe, Ill.: The Free Press, 1956); Graham Wootton, "Parties in Union Government: The Association of Engineering and Shipbuilding Draughtsmen," *Political Studies* (Oxford), Vol. IX (June 1961), pp. 141–56; G. N. Ostergaard and A. H. Halsey, *Power in Co-operatives* (Oxford: Basil Blackwell & Mott Ltd., 1965).

[16] See above, p. 4.

influence upon public bodies. For the moment, however, we accept (not broken-heartedly) a self-denying ordinance.

Granted that Targets must be limited to public ones, what does *public* comprise? The easy answer is in terms of the classical governing bodies: legislatures and executives or administrations. But what, in Europe, of the public corporations or nationalized industries? Some of these may not be closely implicated in public policy (e.g., in France, the Renault car firm), but others presumably have at least the same order of importance in this respect as a "regular" government department (e.g., the Bank of France). The point is well made by the British Post Office's transition in the late Sixties from a government department to a public corporation. Accordingly, what had been automatically within the ambit of interest-group discussions tended, if the conventional focus of the subject were retained, to disappear from sight. A far more important British example, however, is afforded by the National Economic Development Council ("Neddy"), set up in 1962 as part of an attempt by a Conservative government at "indicative planning," and later widely accepted as a permanent feature of the landscape. It has a powerful official complement (the Prime Minister, the Chancellor of the Exchequer, etc.), but also brings together the interest-groups (trade unions, nationalized industries, management generally) which are intended to be influential and seemingly are. On the other hand, the "Neddy" Office is not a government department, though, to make confusion worse confounded, it naturally draws upon public funds. Is "Neddy" *public* in the relevant sense?

The United States is not backward in furnishing its own uncertainties of a related kind, but the crucial instance of the ambiguity of *public* (in *Pub. T.*) is provided by the courts generally and the U.S. Supreme Court in particular. In context, *public* could be replaced by *political*, the referent (or *thing*) of both being in part *public policy* as the "output" of an institution, or the outcome of an institutional process. But many Americans and perhaps most Western Europeans do not perceive the courts as political institutions. In a way, this is a curiously blinkered view, since the courts obviously do shape public policy, however strenuously some of the judges may deny it. In England, for instance, the courts in their treatment of trade unions up to (say) 1909 certainly impinged upon public policy at a high level. The explanation of this blinkered view is to be found partly, as Robert Dahl has suggested,[17] in the widespread failure to recognize that in practice the courts go beyond the purely "legal" criteria (the precedents, for example) into the realm of personal predilections (e.g., *of* English judges toward trade unions). Sociologically, the misconception probably derives from the failure to perceive "law as part of a complex social system, functionally interconnected with every other aspect of society . . . ," as Simpson and Yinger[18] put it. On the other hand, the courts do vary in the extent to which they are accessible to interest-group *initiatives* on public policy. To

[17] Robert A. Dahl, "Decision Making in a Democracy: The Role of the Supreme Court as a National Policy-Maker," in *Readings in American Political Behavior*, ed. Raymond E. Wolfinger (Englewood Cliffs, N. J.: Prentice-Hall, Inc., 1966), Chap. Ten.

[18] George E. Simpson and J. Milton Yinger, "The Sociology of Race and Ethnic Relations," in *Sociology Today*, ed. Robert K. Merton, Leonard Broom, and Leonard S. Cottrell, Jr. (New York: Basic Books, Inc., 1959), p. 390.

these the English courts are usually impervious, and in Britain, accordingly, the "screening-out" of the courts from the political process (and so from our *Pub. T.*) is apt enough. But in the United States the courts can be far more readily selected by an interest-group as a *Pub. T.*, so that litigation, echoing Clement Vose, becomes "a form of pressure-group activity."[19] The stock example is important enough to revive: it consists in the fifty or so successful initiatives (up to 1958) of the National Association for the Advancement of Colored People to improve the legal status of Negroes through the courts. Its efforts culminated, if they did not conclude, in the celebrated Supreme Court decision of 1954 requiring the desegregation of schools.

So it turns out that "public is as public does," on the model of "handsome is as handsome does." In other words, a body (and so a Target) is *public* if, empirically, it has a large public policy-making role. In turn it follows that what has to be included under *Pub. T.* varies considerably from one political system to another. Our choice will be governed by convenience, the nature of our inquiry, and the level of abstraction at which we are aiming. On balance, political scientists still tend to confine themselves to the classical Targets, while giving some attention to the courts, notably the U. S. Supreme Court, but neglecting other "possibles." This is not rejection on principle (e.g., on "essentialist" grounds) but exclusion by default, reflecting a lack of information, which, however, could probably be repaired substantially if we set our minds to it.

Turn, finally, to the G, which requires two points of elucidation, one from Target's standpoint, the other from Actor's. To Target, Actor's claims or demands mean decisions or policies. We should be clear that these are to be interpreted as *within the public-policy domain*. That seems obvious enough, being congruent with *Public Target*, but it is not free from ambiguity. In Britain the restrictive phrase conveniently excludes the efforts of the Civil Service Clerical Association to obtain an increase in salaries, that being only an expression of a collective-bargaining relationship in which the employer happens to be the government. But in the United States, the corresponding efforts of the United Federation of Postal Clerks, the National Association of Letter Carriers, and the National Rural Letter Carriers (e.g., in 1964, to secure the passage of a bill increasing the pay of federal employees) were recorded under the 1946 Regulation of Lobbying Act, and so tend to fall within the scope of the concept. Despite that, the exclusion ought to be sustained, not on "essentialist" grounds but in recognition of convenient limits of inquiry. If so, however, ought we to entertain the influence of business firms on the government for the securing of contracts? Such influence *is* briefly discussed in the next chapter. Everything depends upon the context. Any comparison of the relative influence of unions and of "business" would demand consistent treatment, but in discussing "business" alone, the inclusion of corporate influence as such is more justifiable. Above all, in the

[19] "Litigation as a Form of Pressure Group Activity," in Wolfinger, ed., *Readings in American Political Behavior*, Chap. Eight. See also *ibid.*, Part Three, the articles by Martin Shapiro, Frank J. Sorauf, and David J. Danelski; also Glendon A. Schubert, "The Study of Judicial Decision-Making as an Aspect of Political Behavior," *American Political Science Review*, Vol. LII (December, 1958), 1007–25, for which a handy source is S. Sidney Ulmer, *Introductory Readings in Political Behavior* (Chicago: Rand McNally & Co., 1961), Chap. Six; and Jack W. Peltason, *Federal Courts in the Political Process* (Garden City, N.Y.: Doubleday & Company, Inc., 1955).

particular case discussed in the next chapter, the contracts were of such significance as to impinge upon public policy, which would perhaps be less often true of the collective-bargaining claims.

In terms of the Actor, the *G* takes no account at all of whether he is *self-regarding* or *other-regarding* (a distinction that corresponds in part to the one we saw within *PA* between social groups *of* and social groups *for*). Perhaps it is as well, for the distinction, made by John Stuart Mill, was long ago shown up as untenable. In terms of *meanings*, the actions of bankers at Albany, of wool merchants at Washington, and of anti-slavery propagandists in England and the United States are here read as identical. Accordingly, at *this* level of abstraction, the question of *ultimate* motivation (as judged perhaps by *cui bono?*) simply does not arise. At least, not in the sense of "what pushes" a man; we do consider the immediate "pull"—the goal to be achieved, which is in line with our basic approach: "Meaning, in short, must be analysed by reference to its genesis in a context of purposive behavior."[20] But at our level of abstraction, the Goal is necessarily formal: a certain decision or policy by a certain political institution.

It follows that if the *G* is formal, then what "governs" the concept (= really defines it) at this "end" is not the *G* but the *T*. In other words, we cannot, at this level of abstraction, distinguish interest-groups according to whether they are "selfish" or "unselfish," for themselves or for others. Immediately, and at this level, every interest-group, however saintly, is out for itself, i.e., out to extract a favorable decision from the public authorities. The "quality" of the goal-decision, and of the ultimate motivation accounting for it, we do not attempt to judge. Not because as political scientists we eschew values (which we do not), but because we cannot do our work without abstraction and so without loss of detail, i.e., of content. This does not mean that we are committed to this particular concept for all time. Different "slices" of social reality can always be excised. But we had better see what "patterns" can be made from the existing concept before we discard it.

The concept can now be further cut down in this way:

$$PA \longrightarrow T : G^{21}$$

SYNTHESIS

By dissolving *interest-group* into its component parts, we find that it is comparatively complex. But is not *interest-group* taken as a whole, or unanalyzed, *itself* a component of some larger structure? Yes; *interest-group* is evidently a component of a certain type of society. If we can identify this in outline, we shall have again achieved what some authorities considered to be a kind of real definition.

[20] Abraham Kaplan, *The New World of Philosophy* (London: William Collins Sons & Co. Ltd., 1962), pp. 33–34.
[21] A mnemonic device: "Read" the concept as if you were surprised by the identity of an unexpected telephone caller: "Pat? Gee!"

In order to get our bearings, we may recall the proposition advanced in 1861 by the British jurist Sir Henry Maine—"that the movement of progressive societies has hitherto been a movement *from Status to Contract.*"[22] The contrast was with ancient society, where men's opportunities in life were substantially determined by their status in the family. But over many centuries the bonds of status loosened, and increasingly men learned to "bargain" (or contract) for their positions in society; in this sense men's opportunities in life are in general *proportionately more* dependent upon contract than upon status. Roughly, the contrast is between a social system in which roles are allocated very largely on a basis of ascription ("inheritance" in a very broad sense to include male–female attributes) and one in which role allocation is still partly ascriptive but also and increasingly determined by way of achievement, i.e., by letting talent—a man's attributes and capabilities—find its level. Indeed, a whole area of life—the occupational—opens up in which roles are very largely achieved. If we focused attention upon that area to the neglect of sex attributes, of family and kinship, where roles are still ascribed, we could say that role allocation in modern society relies largely upon achievement, not ascription.

The work of the German sociologist Tönnies (1887)[23] more or less parallels Maine's and is even more apt for our purposes here. His starting-point was a distinction between two types of *will* (roughly translatable here as two types of social motivation), the natural and the rational. Correspondingly Tönnies distinguished two types of social relationship. In the one type, observable in the family, our ends are more diffuse than specific, and we ourselves are treated in the round, for ourselves as whole persons, while the relationship is suffused, so to speak, with a warm glow of affection. In the other type, observable in a factory, we are narrowly regarded, treated not for ourselves as persons but simply as units in a specialized role designed for a specific end, the relationship between persons-in-roles being in principle cool and strictly instrumental (or "strictly business"). Now on that basis two types of society can be distinguished according to the *proportions of* the two types of relationship found to exist in them. In the first, still commonly known by the German term *Gemeinschaft* (or communal society), the more "rounded" type of relationship predominates: this corresponds roughly to Maine's era of status. In the second type of society, *Gesellschaft* (or associational society), the more specialized roles predominate: it approximates to Maine's "contractual" society.

These were illuminating characterizations but hardly discriminating enough. In work extending from the mid-Thirties, the American sociologist Talcott Parsons displayed as with a scalpel different surfaces or facets of Gemeinschaft and Gesellschaft:

1. Are the social relationships broad, leaving the role obligations largely undefined (as in a family, or Gemeinschaft); or are they narrow, typically "put down in writing" (as in business, or Gesellschaft)?
2. Are the social relationships warm and affectionate, or cool and businesslike?

[22] Sir Henry Sumner Maine, *Ancient Law* (London: John Murray, 1924), p. 174. For a criticism of this famous generalization, see Frederick Pollock's Note L, pp. 183–85.
[23] Ferdinand Tönnies, *Community and Association*, trans. Charles P. Loomis (London: Routledge & Kegan Paul Ltd., 1955).

3. Are the "rules" or standards governing the relationships "bent" for particular persons (as in nepotism), or are they applied without fear or favor?

4. Are social relationships defined in terms of some quality ascribed (birth, age, beauty) or in terms of what a person can actually contribute to the enterprise or game?

These make up one version of the celebrated "pattern variables," held to be dichotomous and expressible as:

1. diffuseness   *v.* specificity
2. affectivity   *v.* affective neutrality
3. particularism   *v.* universalism
4. ascription   *v.* achievement
   or quality   *v.* performance[24]

Clearly, these are sharper tools; using them, we can discriminate not only between Gemeinschaft and Gesellschaft but also within Gesellschaft. For instance, Italy, France, Britain, Australia, the United States, and Canada all belong to the Gesellschaft pole or end, but the first three can be shown, *empirically*, to be more particularistic and ascriptive than the last three. Each one in each set, in turn, will differ from its neighbor along these and the related dimensions. Similarly, the "pattern variables" can be used to make distinctions within any one social system, e.g., between the social norms (or values) of the economic order and those of the political order.[25] But for the purposes in hand here, the "pattern variables" are useful for identifying in rather more detail the type of society in which interest-groups flourish. Adding some other elements (e.g., occupations and social-class differentiation) to the "pattern variables," we may contrast (following Francis Sutton)[26] two types of society (to which actual societies approximate in varying degrees):

AGRARIA

1. *Predominant* norms are diffuse, affective, particularistic, and ascriptive.

2. Social structure comprises stable local groups having little mobility.

INDUSTRIA

1. *Predominant* norms are specific, affectively neutral, universalistic, and achievement-directed.

2. High degree of social mobility, horizontal if not vertical.

[24] I omit the self *v.* collectivity dichotomy which Sutton (see note 26) uses but which Parsons has since acknowledged to be a special case, standing on "a more general logical level." See *The Social Theories of Talcott Parsons*, ed. Max Black (Englewood Cliffs, N. J.: Prentice-Hall, Inc., 1961), p. 330. The *locus classicus* is *The Social System* (Glencoe, Ill.: The Free Press, 1951), which should be followed by David Lockwood, "Some Remarks on 'The Social System,'" *British Journal of Sociology*, Vol. 7 (1956), 134–45.

[25] Seymour Martin Lipset, *The First New Nation* (London: William Heinemann Ltd., 1964), p. 212 and n. 8. For other political applications, see n. 9.

[26] F. X. Sutton, "Social Theory and Comparative Politics," in *Comparative Politics*, ed. Harry Eckstein and David E. Apter (New York: The Free Press, 1963), p. 71. The names "Agraria" and "Industria" (adjective: "Industrian") come from Fred W. Riggs, in *Toward a Comparative Study of Public Administration*, ed. William J. Siffin (Bloomington: Indiana University Press, 1959), pp. 23–116. Riggs took over Sutton's characterization and elaborated it in great detail.

AGRARIA *(cont.)*	INDUSTRIA *(cont.)*
3. Occupational differentiation is comparatively simple and stable.	3. Occupational differentiation is well developed and segregated from other structures.
4. Stratification system is diffuse and embodies deferential values.	4. Stratification system is more egalitarian and achievement-directed.
5. Few "associations" separate out.	5. Characterized by "associations," i.e., "functionally specific, nonascriptive" structures.

Crude though this typology admittedly is, it represents a map enabling us to locate interest-groups in a larger structure. Characteristically, the *PA* of the concept constitutes one of the kinds of *association* that flourish in Industria. Since the *T* of the concept constitutes another kind, we see that the interest-group concept (as elucidated) "belongs to" Industrian society (which you will remember to interpret as a constructed type or model around which actual "advanced" societies cluster or range). Accordingly, interest-group activity (as so far isolated) is fundamentally an interaction between associations which flourish in Industria thanks to the prevalence in particular of specific and achievement-directed norms. Whereas ascriptive norms would act as a brake, achievement-directed norms permit associations to be set up at will in order to cope with requirements and problems. At the same time the norms of specificity permit persons to engage "segmentally" in the activities of many associations, i.e., on a narrow "front" and presumably without very deep commitment to any one association.

With this we complete our alternatives to the nominal definitions of *interest-group*. Whether the abstraction and naming, the analysis and the synthesis should be counted as real definition does not, in the end, matter one red cent. What is important is to avoid being forced into a corner at the outset by the sheer weight of the existing definitions, since these apparently encompass *words* not *things*, and *words* whose meanings are simply not consistent. That being so, we abstract the *thing* for ourselves, name it, analyze it, and then place it in context. In this sense, like any other scientific (or systematic) inquirer, we do not *start* with a definition but with value-directed observations (e.g., regarding some public problem or issue) that we endow with meaning.

CLASSIFICATION

Before attempting to reduce the realm of associations to some sort of order, we had better change gear, or shift words. Francis Sutton's "association" is common currency but even in standard works[27] it has been known to include "primary

[27] R. M. MacIver and Charles H. Page, *Society* (London: Macmillan & Co. Ltd., Papermac, 1964), p. 215.

group." In Cooley's classic definition, this was a small group of intimate face-to-face association and cooperation, and so, subject to some revision, it has remained.[28] Certainly it is utterly unlike Sutton's functionally specific, non-ascriptive "association." On balance, "secondary group" finds favor here over "association" in Sutton's sense; this is a post-Cooley notion but implied in his work as a residual category.[29]

How shall secondary groups be classified? Sutton simply distinguished between (a) those "built around occupational participation" (business firms, government agencies, hospitals, universities); and (b) "those built primarily on more limited participation of their members" (the voluntary bodies, such as Protestant churches and patriotic organizations). That hardly suits us here.[30]

What, then, *would* suit us? To begin with, we already have a broad division in the concept itself, between *private (PA)* and *public (T)*. The next step is a classification of groups within the private domain. This is far more difficult. For classification begins as an ordering device but does not end with it. Somehow the categories so ordered have to *mean something*, if possible, to Observer as well as observed. For example, the classification ought to enable us to judge Target's perception of Actor, since that would seem likely to be one of the variables governing Actor's influence upon Target. Now presumably Target's attitude will be the more favorable, the greater Actor's social contribution is perceived to be (Target, of course, being in some sense representative of the society deemed to benefit from Actor's contribution). This leads to a classification bringing into focus Actor's *social contribution*. Other considerations (e.g., why does this type of Actor have access to this Target?) point in the same direction.

If we try out this approach for the private (secondary) groups, we find ourselves turning to *functionalism*, or, even, if determined to live dangerously, to *structural-functionalism*. Highly controversial though these modes of thought remain, they can yield something useful to us here, because, directly or indirectly, they grapple with problems of social contribution. In anthropology, functionalism at its most general has meant the interpretation of a society, or culture, as an organization of means for the achieving of certain ends, whether of individuals or of associations of individuals.[31] In serving the ends (whether biologically or socially derived), the means may be called *functional*: having the

---

[28] C. H. Cooley, *Social Organization* (New York: Charles Scribner's Sons, 1929). The work was first published in 1909. For a revision, see Ellsworth Faris, "The Primary Group: Essence and Accident," *American Journal of Sociology*, Vol. 38 (July, 1932), pp. 41–50.

[29] It is important to realize that every social group has both Gemeinschaft-like and Gesellschaft-like attributes, so that even a family has a touch of Gesellschaft (e.g., it entertains the specific goal of reproduction) and even a factory has more than a touch of Gemeinschaft (in some of the working groups). It is a question, in "live" inquiry, of proportions. Yet in sociological discussion it is very common to ignore the smaller, "dissident" component, and to speak of *one* sort of social group *as if* it had nothing but Gemeinschaft-like qualities, and of another sort *as if* it had nothing but Gesellschaft-like qualities. When we slip into that mode of speaking, we assimilate the former to *primary group*, and the latter to *secondary group*.

[30] Nor does the more systematic (and generally very useful) classification suggested by Blau and Scott. See Peter M. Blau and W. Richard Scott, with introduction by J. H. Smith, *Formal Organizations* (London: Routledge & Kegan Paul Paperbacks, 1966), pp. 42–57.

[31] Robert Redfield, "Relations of Anthropology to the Social Sciences and to the Humanities," in *Anthropology Today*, ed. A. L. Kroeber (Chicago: University of Chicago Press, 1958), p. 734.

observed consequence of contributing to that system of which the ends are in some sense a feature. Much the same notion turns up in sociology, where, however, more thought has been given to specifying the "functional requirements" of the social system under scrutiny, i.e., "the things that have to get done if society is to continue as a going concern."[32] Under various names (social imperatives; functional imperatives or problems; functional requisites; functional exigencies; universal necessities), these have been codified several times and as often criticized. The difficulties are genuine. For instance, how do we judge whether this or that society is a "going concern"? Is Sicily "going"? Hardly, yet the society that is Sicily does jog along somehow. As for survival, we can judge that for an organism, but what is it—and what is death—for a society or social system? In the functionalist canon the sweet simplicity of death is lacking. On the other hand, it is true that in every society certain sets of tasks or activities have to be *tackled* or *undertaken*.[33] Holding on to that, we can explore the ground in two stages, the first keeping close to common sense and by its persuasiveness preparing the way (in effect) to the second, more exotic habitat. Sociologist Kingsley Davis took his stand fundamentally on the necessity of maintaining the population, which requires the provision of nutriment, protection against injury, and reproduction.[34] Now, in principle, apart from reproduction, men and women could try to meet these necessities individually, but in fact they try to do so collectively, through various social arrangements, which, being structured, organized, or patterned, are commonly referred to as the *social structure* or the *social organization* or the *social system*, or even as *the pattern*. Now once that approach has been adopted, the necessities have been correspondingly widened, for the social organization (or system) *itself* now has to be attended to; otherwise the required results cannot be expected. Meeting the fundamental necessities by the collective method *means* subdividing the work and at the same time—the usual paradox—gathering it together again for the attaining of various ends, or goals. It also means keeping in good fettle the members who undertake the work, and seeing that they are sufficiently united or cohesive for the purpose, which might be translated as *keeping up their morale*. More generally, an attempt has to be made to keep a social organization going, for once having chosen (or at least arrived at) the collective way, men and women would be in a desperate situation if they had to try to fend for themselves individually. In this sense we *can* speak of society's, or a social system's, *having needs*, although the usage is risky.

This is one commonsense approach; another is Alex Inkeles's account of the "minimum requirements of human social life."[35] Thus armed we *draw upon*

---

[32] D. Alberle, A. Cohen, A. Davies, M. Levy, and F. Sutton, "The Functional Prerequisites of a Society," *Ethics*, Vol. LX, No. 2 (1950), 100–111; Marion J. Levy, Jr., *The Structure of Society* (Princeton, N. J.: Princeton University Press, 1952); Walter Goldschmidt, *Understanding Human Society* (London: Routledge & Kegan Paul Ltd., 1960), Chap. III. For an application to political science, see Marion J. Levy, Jr., "Some Aspects of 'Structural-Functional' Analysis and Political Science," in *Approaches to the Study of Politics*, ed. Roland Young (London: Atlantic Books and Stevens and Sons Ltd., 1958), pp. 52–66.

[33] Chandler Morse, "The Functional Imperatives," in *The Social Theories of Talcott Parsons*, ed. Max Black (Englewood Cliffs, N. J.: Prentice-Hall, Inc., 1961), p. 144.

[34] *Human Society* (New York: The Macmillan Company, 1948), p. 30.

[35] *What Is Sociology?* (Englewood Cliffs, N. J.: Prentice-Hall, Inc., 1964), p. 64.

the version developed by Talcott Parsons, although without commitment to the celebrated scheme of codification of which it is part, and in the weakened form[36] already indicated. Those words are italicized in order to emphasize that we are borrowing only for the specific purpose in hand—to acquire a classification of secondary groups that highlights *social contribution*. Thus attenuated, one version of the protean Parsonian system can be summarily deployed as follows:

1. Adaptation	3.	Pattern-maintenance and tension-management
2. Integration	4.	Goal-attainment

(1) Adaptation. Of what, to what, for what? *Of* the society, or social system, *to* the social and physical environment. This entails the division of labor, or role specialization, for the production of the goods and services that people need. Obviously a critical area, given the underlying and conditioning fact of scarcity in relation to the gratification of people's needs.

(2) Integration. Of what or whom? Either: the binding together of the roles of the system, or (more loosely) of the persons who perform the roles. This binding together requires certain rules or procedures (social norms), including sanctions for enforcement. But these are enveloped in an ethos or *esprit* that is commonly called morale, solidarity, cohesiveness, or loyalty.

(3) Pattern-Maintenance and Tension-Management. In contradistinction to integration, which has to do with relationships *between* the parts (or roles), this functional requirement focuses upon the parts themselves. It has two facets. On the one side, each part or role (loosely, each person) is expected to learn the values of the social organization (or structure or system), so that it will be perpetuated even though the persons who perform the roles at any given time must eventually die. This, roughly, is the maintenance of the pattern. The process may be conveniently called a socializing, or cultural, one (in the sense of transmitting cultural values—those values, beliefs, and emotions that distinguish one *pattern* or social organization or social system from another).

The other facet touches the condition of the part (or role) in a different sense; here the concern is with the proper functioning of each part—keeping each part "fit" in the widest sense, psychologically as well as physically; restoring it to "fitness" after its subjection to strain and tension. Recreation has its place here, but also the creative arts (sometimes referred to as the expressive function).

(4) Goal-Attainment. Although a society (or social system) may not seem to exhibit any clear sense of direction, it is presumably not drifting. Some joint or collective ends will be pursued, and with some degree of success. We may

---

[36] Following Chandler Morse (in *The Social Theories of Talcott Parsons*), who should be consulted for the references to that part of the Parsonian epic which alone concerns us here. But the threads could be picked up through Talcott Parsons and Neil J. Smelser, *Economy and Society* (Glencoe, Ill.: The Free Press, 1956).

follow the Parsonians in calling this goal-attainment, while acknowledging again that success is problematic or contingent.[37]

Now what we want is to identify the actual social groups responsible for carrying out these four societal tasks, for that would furnish us with some standard of the groups' social significance. The identification, however, is not straightforward, fundamentally because the Parsonian categories cut "diagonally" through the social system, i.e., (a) any *one societal task* is undertaken by *more than one* type of group, while (b) any *one type of group* serves *more than one* societal task. Thus, (a) the goal-attainment (or political) task is not confined to government (a complex of groups), while (b) government undertakes more than the political. All the same, we are permitted to identify such-and-such a group as mainly responsible for such-and-such a societal task, e.g., that government *is* mainly responsible for goal-attainment. This is precise enough for the purpose in hand, yielding four broad categories of groups:

Societal task	Corresponding group, named à la Parsons	Corresponding group, named à la Smelser
1. Adaptive	Adaptive	Economic
2. Integrative	Integrative	Integrative
3. Pattern-maintenance and tension-management	Pattern-maintenance	Cultural (wide sense)
4. Goal-attainment	Implementive	Political[38]

This carries us on to:

Group mainly responsible for carrying out task	Representative examples
1. Economic	Factories, plants, mines, offices, farms; or the legal entities (partnerships, corporations)
2. Integrative	Legal institutions
3. Cultural (wide sense)	Families, churches, schools
4. Political	Legislatures, Executives, including government departments and agencies

[37] This brief account does scant justice to the subtle Parsonian analysis, but then this discussion of mine has its own imperatives.

[38] The names attributed to Parsons are those he used to classify goals and then organizations. See "A Sociological Approach to the Theory of Organizations," in his *Structure and Process in Modern Societies* (Glencoe, Ill.: The Free Press, 1960), pp. 44–47. But for us here the more familiar terms used by the distinguished neo-Parsonian Neil Smelser are more suitable. See *The Sociology of Economic Life* (Englewood Cliffs, N. J.: Prentice-Hall, Inc., 1963), pp. 28 and 37.

As will be noticed, these are almost entirely secondary groups; the significant exception is provided by the family as a species of primary group. That exception apart, "boxes" 1, 2, and 3 house private secondary groups (counting "schools" as part of a large educational system, and so on). These private secondary groups become interest-groups when they exercise ventured influence upon the public (secondary) groups found in box 4.

At this stage, we should acknowledge frankly that we are parting company from the Parsonians, as much for their sake (so that they shall not be mis-represented) as for ours. The point is both general and specific. The general point is that we at least cannot assume that all secondary groups in society fit into one or other of these four boxes. Whether intentionally or not, functionalists do tend to leave the impression that somehow all structures (or groups) "fit in" somewhere, which means in this context that all secondary groups can be related to the societal tasks, and so placed (principally) in one of the four boxes. This can be readily expressed in functionalist language. When a group makes a "positive" contribution to a societal task, as a matter not of subjective purpose or intention but of actual objective fact, empirically determined, it can be said to be *functional for* the system of which it forms part. By contrast, a group that *in effect* hinders the societal work may be called *dysfunctional* (compare *dys-pepsia*). But does this mean that every (interacting) group dotted about the social landscape counts functionally one way or the other? We cannot assume so, since the issue demands observations, not assumptions. In the absence of hard data, we adopt here the commonsense hypothesis (a testable proposition) that some social groups either do not count functionally, or count so little that they can be usefully distinguished from those groups *judged* to bear the main burden of responsibility.[39] Consider such bodies as the Royal Horticultural Society (RHS), which organizes the devotees of the English sport of gardening; the British Psychological Society; the British Academy of Forensic Science; and the British Nuclear Energy Society—all species of the *study association*, further-ing "knowledge of a subject in a narrow field of enquiry."[40] The RHS may well serve pattern-maintenance and tension-management, and so could be classified as *cultural* (in the special sense). But Target can hardly be expected to have the functionalist's all-seeing eye; accordingly it puts the RHS away in the category of the groups that can safely be discounted. This may be unsafe on some occasions; it is always possible, in propitious circumstances, for a group to transcend its category. Targets, however, necessarily have their eyes on the things that loom largest on the ground. As with the *study association*, so with the *prestige association*. The American Philosophical Society and the American Academy of Arts and Sciences may serve pattern-maintenance and tension-management; the Académie Française, with its special concern for the purity of the language and hence for French traditions, might even be regarded as serving integration as well. Yet Target probably neglects them most of the time.

Thus the ambiguity surrounding "count" in "count functionally" above

[39] Adapted from David Lockwood, *op. cit.* (note 24), and T. H. Marshall, *Sociology at the Crossroads* (London: William Heinemann Ltd., 1963), pp. 28–29.

[40] Geoffrey Millerson, *The Qualifying Associations* (London: Routledge & Kegan Paul Ltd., 1964), p. 35.

begins to be dispelled. To the question "Count *to whom?*" the answer now comes: partly to Actor (interest-group) itself, since its functional status goes a long way toward explaining its methods and influence; but also, reading the result at the other end, to Target, which, as the body *mainly* responsible for goal-attainment, has to weigh the claims made upon it by Actors. Such evaluations of functional significance should presumably be "allowed for" in our classification. Here, however, we realize that the penumbra of ambiguity around "count" has not been entirely dispelled, for, as always, there are two levels of analysis, two vantage-points. Target does not see all of the game, and its perception has to be "corrected" by Observer if the workings of a system are to be understood, the advantages and disadvantages of interest-groups properly assessed. That is, some groups may have *functions for* a system that were not intended by them or by anybody, and that have escaped Target's notice. Such functions (or *actual* consequences) have been dubbed *latent*. Their discovery is one of the special responsibilities of the observing political scientist, who has the training and the leisure that Target lacks. Target itself (according to my hypothesis) tends to weigh the claims of interest-groups principally in terms of its judgment of *manifest functions*,[41] those actual consequences that were planned (or appear *as if* planned) and are recognized. Our classification takes that into account, although it does not predetermine the outcome; the classification might usefully survive even if the hypothesis were refuted.

To Target, then, but with indirect meaning for Actor *qua* interest-group, the scene may be laid out along a line representing gradations of functional significance:

Cluster A	*Cluster B*	*Cluster C*
Concrete groups whose contribution to the great societal tasks is manifest to Target	Concrete groups adjudged to have little functional significance	Concrete groups deemed functionally irrelevant

Obviously, finer distinctions could be made; these cut-off points are simply illustrative. The empirical content is a matter for research, but in Cluster A we expect to find the economic, integrative, and cultural groups; in Cluster C, the study associations, the prestige associations, and the like. Now any of the three types of manifestly functional groups in Cluster A can take the role of interest-group, whereupon they may be given the corresponding label, e.g., *economic interest-group* and so on. Our general hypothesis now is that the line of political importance of interest-groups *tends* to follow the contours of *manifest* functional significance.

One heartening sign that we are on the right track is the extent to which (in Industria) various structures of great complexity have come to occupy the social space between the "operational units" of the social system (the economic,

---

[41] Robert K. Merton, *Social Theory and Social Structure*, 2nd rev. ed. (Glencoe, Ill.: The Free Press, 1957), Chap. I.

integrative, and cultural groups) and the public secondary groups (or government). It is as if a multistoried building had been erected on a base formed by the "operational units." Here, however, we cannot do justice to social reality, and have to content ourselves with a gross simplification of it, indicating only two levels of "superstructure," which we label levels 2 and 3.

> *Level 2.* Local, regional, and occupational bodies and federations (including the trade unions as well as the national, or industrywide, trade associations, but excluding the "peaks").
>
> *Level 3.* The "peaks"—e.g., the Associated Chambers of Manufacturers, Australia; the New Zealand Employers' Federation; the Canadian Chamber of Commerce and the Canadian Manufacturers' Association; the Confederation of British Industry (CBI) and the Association of British Chambers of Commerce (ABCC); the National Association of Manufacturers (NAM) and the United States Chamber of Commerce; in Italy, the Confederazione Generale dell'Industria Italiana (Confindustria); in France, the Conseil National du Patronat Français (CNPF); the Bundesverband der Deutschen Industrie (BDI) in the German Federal Republic.

Far too much has been telescoped into level 2; in many systems, *three* tiers above the "operational" ought to be provided for. At the "peak" level, complications have been glossed over. For instance, there are, of course, trade-union peaks to match the employers', but, in the Netherlands, the Stichting voor de Landbouw (Federation of Agriculture) has united both the employers (or farmers) and the unions (of farm workers). However, to allow for these complexities would complicate without advancing this particular exposition, so we have to manage with a three-tiered structure, bearing in mind that the tiers are often interconnected and always represent a kind of pyramiding of private secondary groups, roughly specializations *of* specializations.

The examples given above were economic, but the other operational groups also tend to be built upon. Thus, among integrative groups, the levels of City Bar, State Bar, and the American Bar Association might be identified. In Britain, the operational unit is an Inn of Court, an independent, self-governing "branch" of something like a legal university. It admits one to practice at the Bar, and can also disbar or otherwise discipline. At a higher level stand the General Council of the Bar, which inquires into allegations of unprofessional conduct and recommends appropriate action to the Inn concerned; the Inns of Court Executive Council, which considers matters referred to it, reaching decisions that are binding upon the four Inns; and the Council of Legal Education, which also makes within its range decisions that do not require ratification by the Inns. Functionally, all three, however, would probably have to be placed within the second tier, there being nothing quite like the American Bar Association. With cultural groups, we might separate out the parish churches and local chapels; the several national churches (Anglican, Baptist, etc.); and the British Council of Churches, which in 1967 brought together 27 member churches.

At present it is impossible to say precisely, or even imprecisely, what the dimensions of these "buildings" are; no doubt there will be variations not only between systems but also, within any particular system, between the three possible foundations (economic, integrative, and cultural) for the superstructures. But if the notion of a three-story (or three-tier) structure is acceptable as a first approximation, we require some additional labels. Groups at the second and third levels may be simply called *second-order* and *third-order* groups. In context, the manifestly functional groups—those operational units of the social system—may be called first-order.

Now, any of the three types of group at any of the three tiers may take on the mantle of interest-group, so that we arrive at this classification:

Economic interest-group, first-order, second-order, third-order

Integrative interest-group, first-order, second-order, third-order

Cultural interest-group, first-order, second-order, third-order

Within any category, second- and third-order groups have been commonly thought to be the interest-groups *par excellence*, but that may exaggerate the role of third-order groups (the peaks) and underestimate the role of first-order groups, e.g., the business firm as such.[42] However, second- and third-order groups are doubtless important in the eyes of Target. That importance probably stems from their being perceived as grounded in first-order groups, to which they might even be conceived as making (*empirically*) a contribution. If that were so, second- and third-order groups could be said to be *functional for* first-order groups. Alternatively, we could describe the derivative significance of higher-order groups in terms of anchorage, saying, e.g., that second-order groups are *anchored* in first-order groups.

Our general hypothesis[43] might now be elaborated: the line of importance of interest-groups *tends* to follow the contours of manifest functional significance, including not only the actual operational units, or first-order groups, but also the higher-order groups anchored in these.

It is essential, however, to realize that not all anchored groups are as easily visible to the naked eye as the ones so far pointed out. So what follows is problematic since we cannot be sure that Target's eyesight is a sharp as we like to think Observer's is. We should have to make inquiries of a strictly behavioral kind (i.e., eliciting meanings[44]) before we could confidently proceed. However, the additions about to be made do seem more *meaningful* to Observer at least; i.e., the overall classification is a better predictor of behavior, provides a fuller explanation of why things are as they are.

Think first of the National Federation of Business and Professional Women's Clubs (USA); in France, of the League of Catholic Action and the Association of Women Doctors; in Britain, of the Association of Assistant Mistresses in Secondary Schools, and the former National Union of Women Teachers (whose main goal was equal pay for women teachers). Is there much point in classifying

---

[42] The national union is often thought of as the analogue of the business firm, but in terms of public policy-making it seems more meaningful to classify it as second-order, not first-order, since it hardly "projects" from that operational level toward government. However, the point does not have to be decided for this discussion.

[43] See above, p. 36.   [44] See above, p. 7 n.

these as women's organizations? To perceive them as anchored in one type of manifestly functional group seems more likely to prove explanatory of their actions and influence. If the Indian Workers' Association in Britain is what it appears to be from its title, we might gain more illumination from classifying it as economic than as ethnic or "racial," e.g., when discussing its continuity as a group or its effectiveness. Even if we do not go as far as "reclassifying," we may do well to be sensitive to *anchorage*. That predecessor of the British Legion, the Comrades of the Great War (1917–21), recruited genuine veterans (or ex-servicemen) under its standard, but it would be impossible to explain its emergence and startling growth unless we knew that it was financed by great banking and industrial concerns much perturbed by the apparent Leftward bias of the veterans' movement.[45]

It is also essential to realize that my classification does not match the traditional one, traceable at least to the American political scientist Harwood Childs in 1935, between groups based on "fundamental differentials" such as occupation and those "existing merely to further special ideas or groups of ideas."[46] That is a distinction often made since (usually without attribution to Childs), and is "natural," but not quite *meaningful*, enough. Consider in nineteenth-century Britain the Anti-Corn Law League. That it embodied an idea or cause is obvious; that it attracted wide, if middle-class, support, is true.[47] All the same its roots were deep in certain economic groups—manufacturers who supplied money, energy, and organizing skill. So it was no "mere" cause group; it was anchored, and anchorage explains to a substantial degree its success. It is even less open to doubt that insofar as the Citizens' Industrial Association of America (1903) and the National Industrial Council (1906) were "in the propaganda field,"[48] they should be classified with the NAM, the putative father of each. In the early Sixties, the London Foundation for Marriage Education, a trust which proclaimed the virtues of "mechanical" (e.g., rubber) contraceptives, was established by the Westbourne Press Bureau on behalf of London Rubber Industries (LRI), Britain's largest manufacturers of rubber contraceptives.[49] The Foundation did not disavow its connection with LRI but apparently did not shout it from the rooftops either. The Genetic Study Unit of 1964–65, which campaigned (e.g., by circulating bulletins) against the use of oral contraceptives, also proved to be an emanation from LRI, working through another public relations (PR) firm. In this instance, however, the connection between the Genetic Study Unit and LRI had been concealed.[50] Here again an ostensible idea-group ought to be classified as an economic group via anchorage. Of course, it may be none the worse for that; what is at stake is meaningful classification.

We must not assume, however, that a close relationship is always "parental." In France in the later Thirties, the Confédération Générale du Patronat

[45] Graham Wootton, *Official History of the British Legion* (London: Macdonald and Evans Ltd., 1956), Chap. I; and *The Politics of Influence* (London: Routledge and Kegan Paul Ltd., and Cambridge, Mass.: Harvard University Press, 1963), pp. 102–3.

[46] "Pressure Groups and Propaganda," *The Annals*, Vol. 179 (May, 1935), p. xi.

[47] Asa Briggs, *The Age of Improvement* (London: Longmans, Green & Company Ltd., 1959), p. 314.

[48] Clarence E. Bonnett, "Pressure Groups and Propaganda," *The Annals*, Vol. 179 (May, 1935), p. 7.

[49] *Sunday Times* (London), June 20, 1965.   [50] *Ibid*.

Français (CGPF), predecessor of the present CNPF, worked closely with the Comité de Prévoyance et d'Action Sociale, even to the point of interlocking directorates and apparently some concerted action.[51] But the Comité had been founded (1936) by a right-wing politician to enroll individual employers in a battle against organized labor as well as to run campaigns to improve the business "image." Nor is the parentage always economic: groups may be anchored in the integrative or cultural groups. It would be impossible to explain the Anti-Saloon League's path to victory—the Prohibition Amendment—except in terms of anchorage in the Protestant churches of rural America, which provided money and organization, including the crucially important use of the pulpit as platform and sounding board. In France too, the Secrétariat d'Etude pour la Liberté de l'Enseignement et la Défense de la Culture is anchored in the Catholic Church, for that reason qualifying as a cultural group.

All the same, it does seem that the economic groups are the most fertile of the manifestly functional groups. For example, from one or another of the tiers of economic structure, we see many a PR concern (a subspecies of idea-group) shyly emerging. Business firms have given rise to or supported such bodies as the American Petroleum Institute, the Economic League, and Aims of Industry Limited (the latter two British). Out of the National Farmers' Union in Britain came the Association of Agriculture; of the BDI (Federation of German Industry), the Institute of Industry. This is but the tip of the iceberg, of course; such peaks as the NAM have a prodigious PR output. It seems to be mainly produced, however, within the organization, whereas we are concerned with the "exposed" groups—those we must train ourselves to classify "realistically" or empirically rather than "logically."

Once a realistic classification has been worked out (a task scarcely begun), we shall have corralled, I think, the interest-groups that really matter, year in, year out, in the process of public policy-making in Industria. We shall also have a basis for that comparative study of systems which alone can save us from untenable generalizations drawn from the study of any one of them. Meanwhile we might wish to pay tribute to the ostensible importance of the corralled groups by referring to them as the *core-groups*.

What lies outside the corral? We must remember that our generalization now is that the line of importance of interest-groups follows the *adjusted* contours of manifest functional significance, such adjustment being the result of actual observation and the interpretations of meanings as embodied in a realistic classification. This generalization can be read either as a long-run tendency or taken as a bench mark; in either sense, it obviously requires qualification. Some groups that Target discounts functionally may still enjoy some importance for a time. Consider veterans' associations. A functionalist might squeeze these in somewhere in relation to the great societal tasks, perhaps declaring that they serve (mainly) integration, and should accordingly be classified as integrative. Target, however, appears not to see it in that light. Nevertheless, government everywhere has accorded such associations a place in the sun, seemingly on other grounds.

[51] Henry W. Ehrmann, *Organized Business in France* (Princeton, N. J.: Princeton University Press, 1957), pp. 43–44.

What grounds? Be absolutely clear that we are not attributing to Target the capacity to detect latent functions. Some of the groups in Clusters B and C (page 36) may indeed have latent functions, but that is Observer's judgment, not Target's. It is just that *in specific circumstances* some groups that are neither manifestly functional nor latently functional (in Target's eyes) can yet gain Target's attention and with that the possibility of exercising influence. Such groups may be of any kind whatsoever, but the more important can be accommodated provisionally in two boxes: those in which membership is ascribed and those in which it is achieved. Together these constitute the more important of the *peripheral groups.*

Peripheral Groups. *Of Ascribed Membership.* Among the universal ascriptive statuses (or "positions"), age, sex, and "race" often acquire political significance. In themselves furnishing nothing more than statistical aggregates, such statuses may in certain circumstances be converted into real (i.e., inter-acting) groups pursuing certain political decisions. An increase in the number and proportion of those of pensionable age may precipitate organizations of "Senior Citizens." If the stimulus is sharp enough, organizations may multiply rapidly, claiming Target's serious attention. In Britain the League of Colored Peoples hardly became a household name in the twenty years or so of its existence from the early Thirties. But when the number of colored persons increased from about 100,000 (early Fifties) to perhaps a million (later Sixties), most of them concentrated in five or six great conurbations,[52] "race" promptly became the basis for many interest-groups. The League itself faded away in the early Fifties, but there arose the National Federation of Pakistani Associations; the West Indian Standing Conference, and, in the Midlands, the Caribbean Association; the Indian Workers' Association (if this, following further inquiry were to be classified here and not as economic). Even the American "Black Power" movement took some hold in the form of the Universal Colored People's Association, founded in 1967. With this, however, as still more with the Racial Adjustment Action Society, we begin to move beyond the confines of the interest-group concept as so far elucidated into a realm where the matrix of interest-group activity as such is no longer accepted as legitimate. That is to say, with some such associations it is no longer apt to speak of a group's making claims upon a Target since the purpose seems rather to overthrow it, possibly disposing of the "underlying" social system at the same time. If so, the activity (or behavior) goes beyond that which has been conveniently demarcated for study *in*, and by means of, the interest-group concept.

From the "Monstrous Regiment of Women"[53] many companies and platoons have been formed. Of these, some would be caught in the toils of our functional classification. The residue varies in importance in time and space. The Women's Social and Political Union in Britain and the National American

---

[52] The Greater London area, the West Midlands, West Yorkshire, South-East Lancashire, Merseyside, and Tyneside. It was in the West Midlands that this printed notice, a facsimile of which was given me by a student, appeared during the 1964 general election: "If you want a Nigger Neighbour Vote Liberal or Labour."

[53] *The First Blast of the Trumpet Against the Monstrous Regiment of Women*, the pamphlet published in 1558 by John Knox, leader of the Reformation in Scotland. As against that, he managed to marry twice, the second time to a teenager.

Woman Suffrage Association had their years of glory up to 1918–20, when the male enemy's earlier capitulation had its practical consequence. In the contemporary scene, the League of Women Voters of the United States (that heir to the Suffrage Association) has some importance. But in Target's eyes most women's organizations (of the residual kind) probably appear as women themselves appear–of aesthetic appeal rather than political import. The picture Target has may be not unlike the charming one conjured up by reflection upon that French organization, the Union of Women Painters and Sculptors.

Where "the draft," or conscription, is in force, as very widely when the world is indulging itself in war, the consequential veterans' (or ex-servicemen's) associations may be counted as ascriptive, being ultimately drawn from males (and sometimes females) of a certain age. Otherwise, they may be conveniently placed in the *achieved* category that follows. Either way, veterans' associations have certainly loomed large in Target's eyes. In France, the three considerable associations coordinated in, or through, the Union Française des Associations de Combattants et Victimes de la Guerre have had a powerful influence upon, for example, the rate of pensions.[54] The American Legion has probably been no less effective; its role has been often described. Precisely because Target does perceive such associations as important, they are sometimes caught up in high politics as well as in the more routine, domestic kind. The role of the British Legion in the later 1930's affords a striking example. The 1935 speech in which the Prince of Wales (the later Duke of Windsor) as Patron of the British Legion commended a proposed Legion deputation to Hitler Germany, thus stretching forth "the hand of friendship to the Germans," had wide repercussions. His father, King George V, rebuked him for mixing in politics, especially as the views expressed were contrary to those of the Foreign Office.[55] A Legion delegation went to Germany, however, and was even received by Hitler himself as well as by Himmler, head of the secret police. They were even shown round the concentration camp at Dachau, although the authorities had taken the precaution of replacing the actual prisoners by S.S. (élite corps) men in disguise, from whose appearance the delegation took home rather the wrong impression of conditions at the camp.[56] A more important involvement in high politics occurred in 1938 at the time of the Munich crisis when, at the request of the British Prime Minister, Hitler gave an audience to the President of the British Legion to discuss the provision of a Legion task force for supervising the transfer of Czech territory to Germany.[57]

These were dramatic moments in a "career" generally as comfortably prosaic as that of any other interest-group. And like all veterans' associations, the British Legion must expect to decline in political importance. That is one "negative" reason for saying that these ascribed-status groups are much less important than the core groups. Another such reason is that we must expect even the "racial" or ethnic groups to lose their importance. Even now, within

[54] Jean Meynaud, *Les Groupes de Pression en France* (Paris: Armand Colin, 1958), pp. 75–76.
[55] Graham Wootton, *Official History of the British Legion* (London: Macdonald and Evans Ltd., 1956), p. 178.
[56] *Ibid.*, pp. 184–86.
[57] *Ibid.*, Chap. XXIX.

Industria, they are significant only in a few systems. Subtract these two classes of groups and the remainder will not count for very much.

Of Achieved Membership. Into the category of groups whose membership is *achieved* fall many of the groups traditionally called "idea-groups" but more commonly known nowadays as "attitude groups."[58] Many but *not* all, for those that can be shown *empirically* to be *anchored* would go in with the manifestly functional, e.g., the Secrétariat d'Etude pour la Liberté de l'Enseignement et la Défense de la Culture; in England, the Genetic Study Unit, and the like. So here again we handle a residue, determined not by so-called "logical" classification (interests *v.* ideas, or interests *v.* shared attitudes) thought up in the seclusion of one's study, but by putting on a stout pair of boots (as R. H. Tawney put it), i.e., by empirical investigation.

In a sense, then, we place here the "pure" interest-group, intending, however, no attribution of "impure" to those groups that are anchored in the manifestly functional, which may not deserve the epithet. Perhaps two sorts of pure interest-group are usefully distinguishable. On the one hand are, for example, in Britain: the Anti-Slavery Society for the Protection of Human Rights (1839), descendant of the body mentioned earlier,[59] the National Anti-Vivisection Society (1875); the British Union for the Abolition of Vivisection, Inc. (1898); the Howard League for Penal Reform (1866); the National Society for Clean Air (1899); the National Society for the Prevention of Cruelty to Children, Inc. (1884); the Royal Society for the Prevention of Cruelty to Animals (1824); and the Scottish Society for the Protection of Wild Birds (1927). All or most of these (as inquiry reveals) can be accommodated within the interest-group concept, as the Howard League makes its rationally based representations to the Home Office for this or that reform. On the other hand, there are groups aptly characterized by journalist George Thayer as the "political fringe";[60] we might even say "beyond the fringe." The stock example is still worth citing: the Campaign for Nuclear Disarmament (CND), which flourished in Britain between 1958 and 1961. It was never an organization of a type consistent with the *PA* of our concept here. As for its Target, it had one initially in the government of the day, or

[58] The *locus classicus* is David Truman, *The Governmental Process* (New York: Alfred A. Knopf, Inc., 1955), pp. 33–35. A major subsequent treatment is in Allen Potter, *Organized Groups in British National Politics* (London: Faber and Faber Ltd., 1961). See also Francis G. Castles, *Pressure Groups and Political Culture* (London: Routledge & Kegan Paul Ltd., and New York: Humanities Press, 1967). Truman himself referred (p. 33) to "common habits of response, which may be called norms, or shared attitudes," but curiously enough it was the "attitude" part that caught on. That has been unfortunate, since *attitude* is characteristically a psychological concept, whereas *norm* is more sociological, which is the level at which the discussion of interest-groups has, fundamentally, to take place. Certainly, *attitude* and *group norm* are closely related; for a nontechnical sketch of the interplay between them, see my *Workers, Unions and the State* (London: Routledge and Kegan Paul Ltd., 1966, and New York: Schocken Books Inc., 1967), pp. 18, 91–94, 101–2, 129. Indeed, they may be taken as correlative concepts. But empirically they "match" only in equilibrium; at any given time, the norms will not be "extrapolations" of the several attitudes. Put the other way round, the group norms cannot simply be "reduced" to the individual attitudes—otherwise every sociology teacher would be unemployed. Since every group has norms—that (from one standpoint) is what its "group-ness" consists in—*attitude group* is muddling.

[59] See above p. 11.

[60] *The British Political Fringe* (London: Anthony Blond, 1965), Chap. 8.

Parliament, but the only consistent target throughout (in terms of *meanings*) was the Labour party qua party and possible incoming government. Even "party" is ambiguous; it "really" meant the Annual Conference of the Labour party, the mass party rather than the parliamentary party, which carries one further and further from our notion of Target. The Annual Conference was won over in 1960, but the victory was temporary, even Pyrrhic, since it precipitated a successful counterattack by the Campaign for Democratic Socialism, which was essentially the creation of former Oxford University graduates within the party, and even operated at first from an office-home in an Oxford suburb. The point now, however, is that CND behavior cannot well be "contained" within the interest-group concept as this has been developed over about a century and a half. That also tended to be true of CARD (Campaign Against Racial Discrimination), when, late in 1967, it appeared to fall under the spell of the militants, partly perhaps under the influence of American "Black Power." The moderates found a home in a new body, Equal Rights, which, by contrast, seemed more consonant with the interest-group concept as so far understood.

Whether we reject as material for classification any behavior we scrutinize, or bend the concept to accommodate it, is ultimately a matter of convenience. The question is simply: What behavior do we wish to demarcate for study? Evidently, however, as the concept stands, some of these peripheral groups, of both ascribed status and achieved status, are very peripheral.

For a quite different reason, some authorities (e.g., Harry Eckstein)[61] would object to the subsuming of *attitude group* (or achieved-status group) under *interest-group*. The distinction (a) between groups having a foundation in objective characteristics as opposed to "only" subjective values (or attitudes) does hold promise of usefulness, as does the related distinction (b) between groups pursuing their interests (in the sense of "material interests") and those that are disinterested. In the technical literature, however, these skeins (a) and (b) easily intertwine, since the objectively based groups can be expected to give expression to material interests. Yet, if racial discrimination is treated, as with Jean Meynaud, in terms of social status and morality, then an association of Negroes formed to fight it could be classified as "disinterested" on that basis, but "objective" and "interested" on the other (Ecksteinian) basis.[62] The proposed distinction also tends, as even in Eckstein, to entail an "essentialist" discussion of the meaning of a word, "interests." The alternative procedure worked out in Chapter Two seems far more likely to be productive. It enables us to treat *interest-group* as a handy label whose use should cause no loss of sleep. And when the procedure is followed through, we eventually hit upon a *special kind of* objectiveness: that of (a) the manifestly functional (or actual consequences of action), accompanied by (b) anchorage in the manifestly functional. But according to the attribution-of-*meanings* approach, someone other than Observer (e.g., Target) must be supposed to perceive (a) and (b) if the whole action is to be understood, so the concept here used has a subjective component as well. In that sense the objective/subjective dichotomy is transcended.

---

[61] *Pressure Group Politics* (London: George Allen and Unwin Ltd., 1960), pp. 9–10.
[62] *Nouvelles Etudes sur les Groupes de Pression en France* (Paris: Armand Colin, 1962), p. 17.

DETERMINANTS OF STYLES OF ACTION

That political systems exhibit different styles of interest-group action is clear even to the naked and untrained eye. The explanation of the differences, however, requires more than normal eyesight. We should first distinguish between ultimate and immediate explanations. In the last resort we would explain different styles by deepening and extending the kind of analysis touched upon in the last chapter. This could take two forms. We would point first to the character of the social system that produces the actors, the *PA* and the *T* of our concept. The leading question would be: How far has the social system traveled the *Gesellschaft* road?[1] In answering this, we have to assume that the system has passed the critical point in the *Gemeinschaft–Gesellschaft* continuum where private secondary groups have become significant not only sociologically but politically; otherwise there is, so to speak, no contest, i.e., no interest-group activity worth writing home about. But beyond that critical point social systems are obviously spread out widely. If by a convention they are all called *Gesellschaft*-like, the "pattern variables"[2] have to be used in order to make finer discriminations. Taking into our purview also the "path to equilibrium," i.e., the character (especially the ease) of the transition from *Gemeinschaft* to *Gesellschaft*, we would have on hand the ultimate independent variables. "Ultimate" at least in terms of one mode of analysis and level of abstraction. The presentation could well be made also in terms of another mode of analysis: variations in *the culture*, meaning here:

> . . . patterned ways of thinking, feeling, and reacting, acquired and transmitted mainly by symbols, constituting the distinctive achievements of human groups, including their embodiment in artifacts; the essential core of culture consists of traditional (i.e., historically derived and selected) ideas and especially their attached values.[3]

[1] See above, p. 28.   [2] See above, pp. 28–29.
[3] C. Kluckhohn, in *The Policy Sciences*, ed. Daniel Lerner and Harold D. Lasswell (Stanford: Stanford University Press, 1951), p. 86, n. 5.

45

This would yield another approach, in which we focused less upon the emergent group-forms than upon the concomitant ideas and especially values, both general and specific.

IMMEDIATE DETERMINANTS

For a brief discussion, however, we must lower our sights, focusing upon the more immediate determinants—variations (a) in the components of our concept and (b) in the relevant relationships. So we start again (see p. 27) from $PA \longrightarrow T : G$. It will be remembered that the restriction (not Pol. P.) after PA has been implied throughout. With that in mind and transposing G(oal) into the form of a claim, we arrive at this provisional list of variations:

1. The nature of the Actor (or group) and its claims–goals
2. The nature and distribution of the authoritative public groups that provide the Target, and the nature of the electoral system by which *they* are "provided" and legitimized
3. The nature of the political parties as organizations and as configurations (i.e., one-party, two-party, etc.)
4. The nature and distribution of the other private (secondary) groups within the total social matrix

But these, it may be objected, are "only" group forms: what of "ideas" and their "attached" values? These can be "written into" the groups as their (social) norms, but since 1956 they have often been accommodated within

5. The *political culture*[4]

and dealt with separately. Political culture consists in the ideas and especially their attached values that bear upon (i.e., tend to regulate) the ends (or goals) of political action and the means that may properly be used to pursue them. It is a valuable concept, but its use is not free from danger. First, it tends to "drift" from the level of abstraction appropriate to the other determinants. Second, there is a standing temptation to infer the political culture from some particular structural configuration and then "project" it "forward" again in partial explanation of that configuration. Even though reputable authors have been known to do that, the procedure is obviously circular and to be avoided like the plague. The evidence for the political culture has to be garnered independently of the feature under scrutiny. This, of course, can be done,[5] but in

[4] Gabriel A. Almond is the source for this concept: see "Comparative Political Systems," *Journal of Politics*, Vol. 18 (1956), pp. 391–409. As applied to the types of systems here considered, an instructive follow-up was that of Samuel H. Beer, Adam B. Ulam, Harry H. Eckstein, Herbert J. Spiro, and Nicholas Wahl, *Patterns of Government* (New York: Random House, Inc., 1958). Borrowing from that work via Samuel Beer, I may have been one of the first in the field in England, having adapted the concept for my doctoral dissertation in 1960. This was published in 1963 as *The Politics of Influence* (London: Routledge & Kegan Paul Ltd., and Cambridge, Mass.: Harvard University Press).

[5] See, e.g., Gabriel A. Almond and Sidney Verba, *The Civic Culture* (Boston: Little, Brown and Company, 1956).

some contexts it is in any case more parsimonious and aesthetically satisfying to conceive the political culture as "built into" the several social groups as the social norms—the code "defining the situation," which is learned through socialization and buttressed by sanctions, rewards as well as punishments.

Thus we provisionally identify either four or five immediate determinants of styles of action; they might be regarded as qualitative variables, although so gross, or compound, that they will have to be reduced in due course to more precise variables in the stricter sense. In this book we use them as beacons, guiding exposition and analysis, i.e., throwing some light upon differences between interest-group action in different systems. Again an objector's voice may be raised: are we not about to look so hard at the interplay between these (sets of) variables that we shall shut out what the product of that interplay—some public policy or decision—"does to" the interplay by "bouncing back" on it? In other words, are we not in danger of failing to make place for "feedback," i.e., for public policy not as a mere resultant of such interplay but rather "as a determinant of the interplay itself"?[6] The explanation is that we must keep to the distinction between Actor's standpoint and Observer's. As observing political scientists, we have to try to *define the field* as it appears to the Actor, whether (say) individual firm, trade association, or union "peak." *Field* is peculiarly apt: if we do not care for the sense of a place where a battle is fought, we might, lightheartedly, conjure up the vision of an arena for sporting events. The primary sense of *field*, however, is that of an area of social space visible through the eyes of the Actor. In reconstructing this, we draw upon: (a) experience, which is a compound of earlier observation and reflection, especially what might be taken as a special component of reflection, *empathy*; and (b) the evidence in the particular case. The possibility of error is obvious but perhaps derives less from the achieving of *rapport* (or empathy) than from gaining access to the minute-books and files of the group in order to see how they defined this or that situation, of which there naturally is no full account in their published reports.

With these reservations in mind, we take the perspective of the Actor, some petitioning group or other. The first question posed must be: Where is this issue decided? Now by Actor the distribution of actual (public) decision-making authority has to be taken for granted. In reality, that distribution is, in some small but appreciable degree, always changing, even, by interpretation, in the (so-called) written constitutions, at least over a certain range of decision. Observer also knows that such change is *partly* the cumulative consequence of decisions taken earlier—the "feedback" effect of, and upon, the interaction of public and private (secondary) groups; but that is Observer's later knowledge, not Actor's current perspective and so not part of Actor's current calculations. At any given time Actor must take a static view in which *goal–decision–public body* seem to be so indissolubly linked that to mention one is to imply the others. Mistakes of attribution may, of course, be made, but there must be *some* attribution. This process yields up a Target.

Actor, then, looks out on a field where the public (secondary) groups are already marshaled, and will be impelled toward *one* of these by the nature of its

[6] Harry Eckstein, *Pressure Group Politics* (London: George Allen & Unwin Ltd., 1960), p. 8; Beer et al., *Patterns of Government.*

goals and so the nature of the decision required. This *one* is the *final one*—the actual location of decision-making authority in the particular case; but of course the groups activated or approached en route may be private as well as public. In either case, however, their activation is only instrumental to the winning of the decision. Thus the scene is set. Already, with Actor aligned vis-à-vis Target, a certain mode of action is tending to emerge, or is at least implied, but the general style that distinguishes one system from another is a product of all the variables. In order to illustrate the interplay of variables, let us take the limited but still sufficiently complex case of two systems, the United States and Britain. At once the problem of comparability arises: How can we ensure that we are comparing like with like, especially if we wish later to raise (at least) the question of measuring interest-group influence? The correct answer is that we cannot *ensure* comparability but we can, in some cases, keep *in*comparability within acceptable limits of error. The method for attempting this falls for discussion in the next chapter. Accept now (on trial, not authority) that one way of keeping incomparability within tolerable limits (when making intersystem comparisons) is to focus upon the same type of Actor, operating upon the same level (first, second, or third order), pursuing a goal that leads to the same type of Target. Such matching is at present difficult to accomplish, the splendid international conferences on the comparative study of interest-groups having yielded more diffused enthusiasm (and personal friendship) than systematic research. For part of our discussion, however, the campaigns of some American and British corporations in the 1960's to win certain aircraft contracts have been sketchily adduced. Such cases are perhaps to be welcomed the more in view of the relative neglect[7] of business corporations as distinct from industry trade-associations and "peaks."

In trying out the schema, we take a leaf from the economist's book and distinguish between short-run and long-run situations. In this particular example of the short-run case the impact of Variable 4 is neglected.

IN THE SHORT RUN

Variable 1. Nature of the Group. Given the other compound variables, the nature of the corporation itself tends to impose a certain style, or pattern, in methods. Like any other interest-group of any importance, a corporation has a characteristic pattern of endowments that may be converted into methods, and certainly sets outside limits to these. Such endowments must not be confused with the totality of factors that may be held to account for a corporation's success in ventured influence, for that assessment brings in "external" factors such as the perceptions and evaluations of those who exercise public authority. Here the question is: What does a corporation have *at its disposal?*

In answering this question, we have to distinguish between gross endowments and net endowments. The endowments of a core group are "intended" for the carrying out of its basic societal task, and so cannot be regarded as

[7] Morris Davis, "Some Neglected Aspects of British Pressure Groups," *Midwest Journal of Political Science*, Vol. VII, No. 1 (February, 1963).

automatically available for conversion into methods. In gross terms, a corporation has three main endowments: a bureaucracy in the technical sociological sense of a formal structure and a precise differentiation of roles authoritatively organized, the operating criteria being both affectively neutral and universalistic. Within this authority structure, the line and staff arrangement would seem to be especially important. Second, it has financial resources that are commonly substantial and may be great or even fabulous, and goodwill (in the accountancy sense) that may be drawn on for credit. Such resources belong of course to the owners (= stockholders, shareholders), but, thanks to the marked tendency in modern industry for control to be separated from ownership, they are in practice at the disposal of the top bureaucracy, either the board of directors or more probably the "operating" managers. Moreover, by the very fact of discharging a basic societal task, these resources are constantly being replenished. Third, a corporation harbors technical knowledge which is in some degree specific or even exclusive, and which may be brought to bear in one way or another. No doubt there are other potentialities; for example, a corporation has employees who may on occasion be mobilized, but in unionized economies this cannot be relied upon as a resource at the corporation's disposal. True, a corporation and its employees may join hands from time to time, in order to fight off a threat of foreign competition[8] or a government proposal that would cause "redundancy"[9] (the new glossy name for unemployment), but no corporation could rely upon this in its forward planning.

In any case, even the other endowments are only gross, not net. From these we have to "deduct" the endowments that are not *versatile*, i.e., readily convertible into methods. Technical knowledge is one such; its possession partly explains the perceptions and evaluations of the corporations by those in positions of public authority, and so goes some way to explain corporate influence. But in itself it is not very versatile. Bureaucratic organization, on the other hand, even allowing for the dysfunctions,[10] is readily adaptable to ventured influence, while in itself money, of course, is supremely versatile—a flying broomstick of a resource. These constitute the corporation's net endowments, the possible "inputs" available for conversion into "outputs," i.e., methods.

Net endowments, then, are what the corporation finds at its disposal for ventured influence. But how much it will allocate to methods, and with what "intensity" any allocation made will be applied (in gentlemanly fashion, vigorously, ruthlessly), are quite different questions.[11] Here we are in the realm of social norms. To some extent, of course, the corporation's choice is circumscribed. Thus, in the United States, a business corporation cannot legally spend money on all ventured-influence procedures, not, e.g., on campaign contri-

---

[8] Robert A. Dahl, "Business and Politics: A Critical Appraisal of Political Science," *American Political Science Review*, Vol. LIII (March, 1959), p. 19.

[9] E.g., on January 14, 1965, aircraft workers marched through Central London to demonstrate in Hyde Park in favor of TSR-2 (*The Guardian*, January 15, 1965). TSR-2 was a supersonic tactical strike reconnaissance aircraft, the alternative to which was then the American TFX (see below, p. 53). The TSR-2 project, however, did not survive.

[10] Robert K. Merton, *Social Theory and Social Structure*, rev. ed. (Glencoe, Ill.: The Free Press, 1958), p. 51.

[11] Another is the efficiency with which any given allocation is made use of. But this has less to do with styles of action than with comparisons of influence. See below, Chapter Five.

butions. Given the will, however, apparent restraints can be overcome; ingenuity (like love) may conquer all. Thus the social norms of the corporation are really the key to allocation and intensive use, especially as the campaign contribution constitutes, in any case, only one method.

How far a corporation will be free to "express itself" (in its net tendencies) in terms of methods is another matter: that depends upon the other sets of variables. But up to a point corporations in different systems seem likely to use methods of a roughly comparable kind. Suppose we put this to a crude test, using the factor *"nature of the group"* to explain intersystem similarities, and then the other factors to explain differences.

The first step is to think what a corporation's net endowments signify in terms of methods: What style do these endowments tend to induce? The net endowments (we hypothesized) were bureaucratic organization (including skills) and money, which we expect companies to allocate freely to ventured influence, and apply vigorously if not aggressively. But to do what? Here we have to separate out (a) particular emphases *within*, from (b) universal aspects *of*, bureaucratic organization. In carrying out its societal task a corporation is already tooled up for substantial or heavy advertising and public relations. Now these activities are, of course, closely connected. As the distinguished British industrialist Sir Miles Thomas put it:

> In forty years of business experience, during which one must have been responsible for buying advertising space worth millions of pounds and mounting innumerable public relations campaigns one comes to the irrevocable conclusion that advertising and public relations are interdependent. They cross-fertilize each other. Separated, or used in isolation, they lose tremendously in impact.[12]

True, advertising and PR are not identical, the latter being very broadly conceived to take in the creation, maintenance, or enhancement of a good name. But there is a kind of *parallelism* between them, not only in objective ("aids to persuading customers to buy the goods"[13]), but also as activities, just as there is also parallelism between these and political PR. For this the base exists: in the United States in 1955, for example, it is estimated that 5,000 firms were running PR departments at an annual cost, for supervisory staff alone, of some $400 million.[14] Given such a base, the marginal cost of embarking upon political PR should be low. Even where the work is farmed out to independent specialists, the marginal cost may be low if the subscription is tax-deductible. Moreover, firms have the appropriate social norms for at least a vigorous use of political PR, whereas some groups (e.g., *some* professional bodies) have inhibitions about it. All these instances constitute aspects of parallelism, which, seeming to be more powerful in firms (and business organizations generally) than in other types of groups—even other types of economic groups such as trade unions—should produce a powerful "natural" tendency toward political PR. How far does observation support this expectation?

[12] *The Times* (London) Supp., "Aspects of Advertising," May 21, 1964.
[13] Sir Miles Thomas, *ibid.*
[14] *Fortune*, November, 1955, cited in Stanley Kelley, Jr., *Professional Public Relations and Political Power* (Baltimore: The Johns Hopkins Press, 1956), pp. 11–12.

Consider the efforts of certain American and British companies between about 1959 and 1967. The goal (and so the scope) of their ventured influence was about the same: the winning of aircraft contracts. This indicated the same type of Target, the administration: in the United States, the Defense Department and the President; in Britain, the Ministry of Technology and the Cabinet. On the American side the principal Actors were the Boeing Aircraft Company, the Western Electric Company, and General Dynamics Corporation. On the other side of the pond, the British Aircraft Corporation fought Hawker Siddeley Aviation in 1967 over the contract for an aircraft for British European Airways (BEA), while Boeing looked on from the side (BEA having originally wanted the Boeing 727-200).

As expected, all the protagonists made a highly professional use of political PR,[15] both in substance and timing. In 1959 the Boeing Company's Bomarc anti-missile (favored by the Air Force) was competing with Western Electric's Nike-Hercules (the Army's choice): at the very time when the relative merits of these anti-missiles was a congressional issue, both companies advertised their wares in the Washington D.C. press. In taking such an initiative the Western Electric Company is known to have been prodded by the Army. So it is no surprise to find in February, 1961, by which time the Army's choice had fallen on Nike-Zeus, that the whole issue of *Army* (the monthly publication of the Association of the United States Army) was given over to its praise, or that four of the seven articles had been written by *serving* army officers.[16] In the same issue, the Western Electric Company and eight of its associated subcontractors took full-page advertisements, complete with a map, recording how much money under the original contract had been spent in each of thirty-seven states.

The 1967 battle between Hawker Siddeley Aviation and the British Aircraft Corporation to secure a BEA contract concerned a civil aircraft, but the British government came into it because BEA is a public corporation (to whose head ministerial "directions" can, in the last resort, be given) and because the government would be footing part of the development costs whatever the aircraft chosen. The Cabinet decision in December was preceded by months of lobbying, which culminated in an astonishing advertising campaign in the national press that irresistibly reminded one of the campaign mounted by the American aircraft companies seven or eight years earlier. BAC's intervention was the more conventional; in full-page advertisements in the prestige newspapers it identified its famous products (e.g., the Viscount, Britannia, VC-10) and the "Return on National Investment" these had procured in the form of export sales and of "prevented imports," a total gain to the British balance of payments of the order (it claimed) of £1,100,000,000. Its experience (the advertisement concluded) was "unique," its reputation "world wide."[17] Hawker Siddeley's response "in an unprecedented series of full-page newspaper advertisements"[18] was the more overtly political, both in timing (two days before the expected date of the Cabinet decision and four days before the actual one) and in content. We have

---

[15] Under which I include political advertising.

[16] Douglass Cater, *Power in Washington* (London: William Collins Sons & Co. Ltd., 1965), p. 41.

[17] *The Times*, November 27, 1967.

[18] Comment in *The Times*, December 11, 1967. See also the "quality" Sundays the previous day.

to recall here that the rivals of a British aircraft company are never confined to Britain; always ready to challenge is the Boeing Aircraft Company, whose 727-200 BEA had proposed to buy, only to run up against the British government's veto. So Hawker Siddeley now felt in a position to point out that, thanks to devaluation and so an increase in the price of the 727-200, the cost per seat-mile of its aircraft would now be some 5 per cent better than Boeing's. But for us the most interesting feature was the company's willingness to grasp —and display—the nettle of public policy. In refusing BEA permission to buy the Boeing 727-200, the Minister of Aviation[19] had agreed to pay the development costs for "extending existing types" of British aircraft to make them more suitable for the 1970's. But BAC (it argued) had designed "a new aircraft (not 'an extension of an existing type')"—a reminder of what government spokesmen had declared government policy to be. Correspondingly, the development costs to be borne by the taxpayer would be six or seven times as great as its own would be.

To this extent observation matches expectation. But, you will immediately object, surely groups other than business corporations (e.g., the American Medical Association) run political campaigns? If so, how does this brief sketch of these aircraft companies' short-run political campaigns advance the argument? It is indeed true that other types of groups do resort to political campaigns, if in widely varying degrees. The suggestion, however, is that political PR is a method induced in particular by the very nature of a company *qua* company (in a certain era). If this were true, we should expect in the long run to find (a) proportionately far more of it by corporations than by any other *type* of group, and (b) a "cumulative" effort at different levels, since, more than any other type of first-order group, corporations grow "outward" and "upward." So to press the point home we need to take a longer time-perspective. This must wait, however, until another aspect of this short-run action has been sketched in.

So far we have used the factor "nature of the group" to explain *some* similarities in the methods used by certain corporations in the United States and Britain on particular occasions. But even a cursory examination of the campaigns reveals differences as well as similarities. One such difference is peculiarly relevant. BAC's and Hawker Siddeley's pre-advertisement efforts had been intensive, but, so far as we know at present, did not match, for example, General Dynamics' Convair Division's use early in 1961 of the congressman for the Fort Worth, Texas, district in which it was situated, Representative James Wright. The immediate goal was to persuade the incoming Kennedy administration that the B-58 bomber, made by Convair at Fort Worth, should not be phased out. Wright (also a Democrat) tried to persuade the Air Force Chief of Staff, then the formidable General Curtis LeMay, that the B-58 was strategically necessary. He also testified before committees of the House and Senate, Convair experts being ensconced, it is said, in his office, presumably to prepare briefs and answer questions.[20] The whole attempt ultimately failed. However, it probably in-

[19] By this time absorbed into the Ministry of Technology.
[20] Cater, *Power in Washington*, p. 39.

fluenced the outcome of the battle, joined in late 1962, between General Dynamics and the Boeing Company. The prize was nothing less than the contract for the hybrid TFX fighter-bomber (much better known under its later title, F-111) distinguished technically for its variable wing design, and, administratively and financially, for its contribution to the cause of "commonality" (one model for general use). Although an official selection board had recommended that the contract should be placed with the Boeing Company, General Dynamics (Convair), aided by the Grumman Aircraft Engineering Corporation, Long Island, N.Y., proved to be the main beneficiary.

Variable 2. Nature of the Target. The most obvious starting-point is to bring into view the congressional committee before which Representative Wright appeared. The general comment was made three generations ago by Woodrow Wilson in his doctoral dissertation—the committee system facilitates lobbying. Lobbyists, he explained, cannot buy whole legislatures, but . . . , which was unkind but perhaps not unkinder than the facts warranted in his day. The key, in any case, is the way in which the committees work, notably through the system of *hearings*. It is the business methods of Congress, as Sir Denis Brogan has said,[21] that constitute the significant difference, the British Parliament having no real parallel to the system of hearings.

The availability, then, of certain "facilities" in the public-institutional arrangements partly accounts for one frame of the pattern, but in the United States the constituencies would also seem to carry more "punch" than they do in Britain. Of course, in Britain, as in any representative system of the liberal-democratic kind, M.P.'s do fight on behalf of their constituents. The M.P. (and a Labour one to boot) who was jokingly called, after World War II, "the member for Austin's" (the great car manufacturers, later absorbed into the British Motor Corporation, now British Leyland) differed from other M.P.'s partly in the degree and proportionate importance of manufacturing specialization in his constituency, and partly in his having been given such a name. In attempts to prevent the closure of certain railways (intended to reduce the vast losses incurred by British Railways, the operating authority), Conservative M.P.'s in the late 1960's were said to be queuing up outside the Ministry of Transport. In the same period M.P.'s for mining constituencies crossed swords with their own Labour government over a similar issue: the closure of unprofitable pits. One even speaks in Britain of "a good constituency M.P." This is often a left-handed compliment, implying that he is totally undistinguished, or even totally useless, at anything else, but within these limits it is a term of approbation. On the other side of the coin, the American congressman may not be responsive "across the board." Angus Campbell and his colleagues have shown that on civil rights the congressman's perception of his district's view *is* pre-eminently important, but on issues of social welfare his *own* attitude is the more signifi-cant.[22] Still, after the last qualification has been made, it remains true that

[21] *An Introduction to American Politics* (London: Hamish Hamilton Ltd., 1954), pp. 349–50. See also M. J. C. Vile, *The Structure of American Federalism* (London: Oxford University Press, 1961), pp. 91 and 100.

[22] Angus Campbell, Philip E. Converse, Warren E. Miller, and Donald E. Stokes, *Elections and the Political Order* (New York: John Wiley & Sons, Inc., 1965), pp. 364–66.

American congressmen do "jump to it" under local influence far more than British M.P.'s do. They "jump to it" because, as sociologist Edward A. Shils has written, they are subject to exceptional strains. Some of these are general but others are experienced in the constituencies, where they occupy positions that are exposed to every wind that blows. For the wind that matters here we revert to Campbell et al. They found that although individuals do, of course, write to congressmen, communications generally come from organized groups, among which economic interest-groups are prominent.[23] The immediate explanation of this relatively greater responsiveness to local influence falls into two parts, which may be called situational and normative.

Variable 3. Nature of the Parties. The situation in which a congressman finds himself in his constituency is that, in Shils's words, "he is very much on his own." That he is so is a consequence of the character and organization of American political parties. These are well known to be mechanisms that emphasize winning public office at the expense of, or at least with scant regard for, general party doctrine. As principally electoral mechanisms, they naturally gravitate to the locale where elections flourish most: in the districts within the counties within the states. That is to say, party organization is decentralized to the extent that the rule is pretty well "every candidate for himself," for which the nearest parallel in Britain is perhaps the campaign of an Independent candidate during a general election. Within the general decentralization, that of the nominating process has been held by David Truman to be peculiarly significant.[24] Here again, as along other dimensions, the differences between the two systems probably have been exaggerated,[25] but there can scarcely be any doubt, after the balance has been struck, that congressmen are at risk in their constituencies to a degree not experienced by M.P.'s in Britain.

In such a situation, a congressman has to be, as Shils wrote, "hypersensitive to the faintest whisper of a constituent's voice"[26] if he is to survive. "Hypersensitive" is probably not too strong.[27] Similarly, a congressman must please. In relation to our discussion of some defense contracts, the point emerges from a remark about Georgia attributed to a senior military officer: "one more [military] base will sink the state." He did not mean that Destiny had been making amends to Georgia (founded as a refuge for debtors), but only that the chairman of the Armed Services Committee in both houses of Congress

23 *Ibid.*, pp. 368–69. Shils's discussion is "The Legislator and his Environment," in *Introductory Readings in Political Behavior*, ed. S. Sidney Ulmer (Chicago: Rand McNally & Co., 1961), pp. 85–94.

24 "Federalism and the Party System," in *Federalism Mature and Emergent*, ed. Arthur W. MacMahon (New York: Doubleday and Company, Inc., 1955), partly reproduced in *American Party Politics*, ed. Donald G. Herzberg and Gerald M. Pomper (New York: Holt, Rinehart & Winston, Inc., 1966), Chap. 3.

25 See, e.g., Austin Ranney, *Pathways to Parliament* (Madison: University of Wisconsin Press, 1965), *passim*, and Jorgen S. Rasmussen, "Party Responsibility in Britain and the United States," *Journal of American Studies*, Vol. I, No. 2 (October, 1967), pp. 233–56.

26 In *Introductory Readings in Political Behavior*, p. 87.

27 Over and over again during the sales-tax debates in Massachusetts in 1965, Democratic legislators who were voting for the tax against official party policy patiently explained to me that *their* constituents were expressing themselves in favor of it. In private their Democratic colleagues were philosophical about the defections, also patiently explaining that no representative was expected to commit suicide.

happened to hail from that state. Local benefit, too, was a theme of Western Electric's advertisement.[28] In sum, a congressman just is more vulnerable than a British M.P.

Variable 5. The Political Culture. And yet: is "vulnerable" entirely apt? Would not some such word as "amenable" capture more of the reality? In a sense it is less a congressman at risk than the behavior appropriate to a congressman. A congressman is more responsive to local influence than a British M.P. partly because his constituents expect far more of him, and partly because he thinks it *right* to be so. Here we are in the realm of the normative.

Again, the contrast is easily exaggerated, but there can be little doubt that many more British M.P.'s than American congressmen define their role in Burkeian terms—that a representative owes his constituents not only his industry but his judgment, and that he betrays instead of serving them if he sacrifices that judgment to their opinion. "Sacrifices" needs to be stressed, for Burke was not claiming complete insulation from constituency views, to which, indeed, he was prepared to give serious consideration. What he was not prepared to do was to sacrifice his considered views merely to please his constituents. If there are some Edmund Burkes on Capitol Hill, they are not going to risk sacrificing themselves by disclosing their identity, at least not back home. But the point, rather, is that such congressmen would be mavericks, having somehow escaped branding by the common socialization processes to which we are, in varying degrees, heir, and of which we are both products and beneficiaries.

These reflections simply amount to first approximations offered to account for some ostensibly different behavior on the part of corporations when undertaking ventured influence on a particular occasion (the apparent facts having been accepted at their face value for the sake of illustration). Suppose we now dig a little deeper.

Turn back to what was written in terms of Variable 2, the nature of the Target (see p. 53). It was true enough up to a point, but in a sense neither the committee system as such nor the method of hearings is fundamental; in the last resort, it is the place of Congress in the whole complex of public institutions that is crucial. In other words, as with Sir Denis Brogan,[29] we turn to the separation of powers, adding that it is this that counts in the last resort. Now, in the particular instance (the award of the aircraft contract), the decision was in the hands of the administration. But if a legislature has autonomous power, its very importance almost prescribes that it will be used instrumentally too, i.e., as a vehicle for influencing the current Target. At least its importance permits or encourages that. Despite the trend toward executive leadership, Congress still enjoys such autonomous power, whereas Parliament does not. This gives the United States what I call its *double-jointed* attribute; i.e., the parts of its system are so articulated as to allow an exceptional degree of movement for each one, so that today's Target is tomorrow's instrument, and today's instrument tomorrow's Target. So one expects Congress or some significant section of it (e.g., one or both of the two Armed Services Committees, or the Appropriations Committee) to surpass Parliament in the frequency, extent, and "productivity" of

---

[28] See above, p. 51.   [29] *An Introduction to American Politics*, p. 349.

its mobilization for ventured influence, indirect as well as direct. This is not to ignore much parliamentary *activity* of the relevant kind, some of which is productive. It is merely to give weakness its due.

"Localism" was provisionally explained, under Variable 3, in terms of the character and organization of American political parties, and the connection between that and some aspects of American elections was lightly touched upon. But cannot such phenomena themselves be seen as dependent, not independent, variables? We could indeed relate them to a seemingly more fundamental feature of the American system: the *division* of powers between the center (where, of course, powers are said to be *separate*) and the "outlying" units, which, as coordinate governments acting directly on the people, constitute for such authorities as Sir Kenneth Wheare the true federal principle. At all events, this division by whatever name has a profound effect upon the whole bent and "feeling tone" of American interest-group politics. It is not simply that the division makes available many more Targets to tempt Actors into action. It is not simply that each Target (state government as a whole) also has *its* powers separated, so that there are state governors, legislatures, and judiciaries to parallel the federal set. It is also that as a consequence of both these arrangements, *double-jointedness* is permanently reinforced. Thus state legislature can be used instrumentally against state governor, and state government as a whole can be harnessed in the pursuit or implementation of a nationwide policy. Thus the corporations and other business groups, especially after World War II, crusaded at both state and federal levels against the union shop.

Now, the division of powers not only explains sectionalism and localism, but even goes a considerable way toward explaining the decentralization in power and structure of the political parties. Thus, as a closer approximation, the two sets of phenomena previously identified, very roughly, as dependent variable (localism) and independent variable (character and organization of the parties) might both be said to derive from a third variable: the division of powers, or the federal principle as such. By contrast, Britain, if taken to mean the United Kingdom, has at present only the special case of Northern Ireland, with its separate Parliament and government but concurrent representation at Westminster, to detract from its unitary constitution. This, other things (as usual) being taken as equal, sets up a centralizing tendency.

Re-examining the social norms of congressmen, we perceive that these require illumination from the wider political culture. Even a sketch of this would almost be a history of the United States; it may be simply equated, following De Tocqueville, with the sovereignty of the people. This, he wrote, has been found, more or less, at the bottom of almost all human institutions, but concealed from view, and often abused, whereas

> In America the principle of the sovereignty of the people is not either barren or concealed, as it is with some other nations; it is recognized by the customs and proclaimed by the laws; it spreads freely, and arrives without impediment at its most remote consequences.[30]

[30] *Democracy in America*, ed. Henry Steele Commager (London: Oxford University Press, World's Classics, 1946), p. 51 (Chapter IV).

Consistent with that, although "patchy" in actual development, is the historical fact (often overlooked by Europeans) of some manhood suffrage dating from before the battle of Waterloo. That is to say, about a decade and a half or more before De Tocqueville visited the country, six Western states (1812–21) had reached something like manhood suffrage (for whites, naturally), while four of the older states had virtually dropped their property qualifications (1818–21). Britain came to manhood suffrage only a century or so later (1918). No doubt that contrast is too sharp, the British miner and agricultural laborer having, with effect from 1885, joined the town laborers (enfranchised in 1867) within the pale of the constitution. But even after 1885 four adult men out of ten had no vote, and overall the difference in the political experience of the two countries is marked. Already in 1828 the number of Americans *voting* (1,155,000) far exceeded the total number *qualified* to vote in Britain (some 652,000) in 1833, that is, even after the First Reform Act of 1832 had increased the electorate by about 49 per cent. Nor, of course, was that difference erected on the base of a larger population: on the contrary, white Americans numbered some 10.5 millions in 1830,[31] as against the British 16 millions a year later. Between 1828 and 1848, the number of voters in the United States trebled (as the population about doubled), but even the earlier total still exceeded the whole British electorate (some 1,056,000) as late as 1866. If we took the American experience and what it must imply in terms of voters' *and* politicians' expectations over something like a century and a half, together with the views of perceptive observers of the American scene, and the "harder" evidence of contemporary research, then (in a way not attempted here) we could gradually paint a picture of American political culture that is not derived from the phenomena to be explained: the instrumental use of congressmen by corporations and their predisposition to be so used.

Here we seem about to explain certain institutional features in terms of an ostensibly more fundamental political culture. This would be consistent with the type of explanation worked out for Britain in 1958 by Harry Eckstein in the spirit of Samuel Beer's[32] adaptation of political culture to the comparative study of European government. In explaining Cabinet stability in Britain and the (so-called) effectiveness of British parliamentary government in general, Eckstein singled out two factors, cultural and structural. The former comprises a conception of political authority that confers greater scope for independent initiatives (for *governing*) than in the United States, greater indeed (according to Eckstein) than in any other democratic country. The structural factor is the strong two-party system. But (he continues) these factors are themselves derivative. The conception of political authority derives from that social deference to which Bagehot drew attention over a century ago as the key to the successful working of the British political system.[33] The strong two-party system draws (it is said) partly on that "habit of deference," partly on some other sources, but mainly (Eckstein concludes) on "the spirit of British politics," specifically its political pragmatism,

---

[31] With the colored population, the American total reached 12.8 million. For the suffrage figures, see Richard Hofstadter, *The American Political Tradition* (New York: Vintage Books, Inc., 1948), p. 50.

[32] In Beer *et al., Patterns of Government*, Chapter 3 and Part Two.

[33] *The English Constitution* (London: Oxford University Press, World's Classics, 1945).

or virtual immunity to doctrine.[34] Thus, in the last resort, the explanation sought is wholly cultural.

Our concern here is less with the content of this explanation[35] than with its type. If followed, it would entail "reducing" Factors 2, 3, and probably 4 of our provisional list to Factor 5 only. Thus, in the American instance, even our "second-stage" explanation invoking the separation of powers and the division of powers might be telescoped into an American cultural value, say, *the over-riding importance accorded weak government*, or at least (if that is obsolescent) a *"general suspicion"* of executive government (such as an English M.P.—in 1717—saw "interwoven" in the British Constitution). Ought we to "reduce" our list in some such way as that? The prospect is attractive. That Variable 5 is on a level of abstraction different from the other variables has already been re-marked upon, so the "reduction" would produce a result not only more parsimonious but more aesthetically satisfying. All the same, the adoption of the procedure for introductory discussions would entail at least two risks, one general, the other specific. The general risk is the ever-present one of getting caught in the trap of circularity. The British politician L. S. Amery, on whom Eckstein largely relied in this context, came perilously close to it if he was not actually caught. He contrasted to the British conception the "prevalent con-tinental conception, derived from the French Revolution, of political power as a delegation from the individual through the legislature to an executive de-pendent on that legislature. That conception naturally involves the widest freedom in the citizen's choice of party regarded as an end in itself." Hence the "almost indefinite multiplication of parties" *as well as* the adoption of systems of proportional representation, commonly based on party lines.[36] In other words, the Amery model is of this kind:

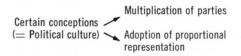

Certain conceptions
(= Political culture)
Multiplication of parties
Adoption of proportional representation

Resisting (with a struggle) the temptation to discuss the adequacy of that model in the light of comparative political sociology, we note that if the contrast is to stand, the British conception of political authority (or political culture) must also be treated as in some sense "causal." But where does Amery find the evidence for that conception of authority? He seems to take it neat *from* British political institutions and practice, supposedly the products *of* the conception.

---

[34] *Patterns of Government*, p. 73.

[35] As a tool of contemporary analysis, *social deference* ought to be examined very critically. Bagehot was writing before the introduction not only of state secondary education in 1902 but also of state elementary education in 1870. One wonders whether *social deference* is not another of those concepts mainly applicable to the Home Counties, i.e., the English counties adjoining London. This is not to deny *strong leadership* as a cultural value, but only to question how far social deference can explain it. May it not have a much more "rational" foundation?

[36] *Thoughts on the Constitution* (London: Oxford University Press, 1947), pp. 17–18.

Of course, the discussion need not be fudged in that particular way. If we are delineating the contemporary culture, we can always *ask*. And Gabriel Almond, author of the landmark article, has with various colleagues but especially Sidney Verba[37] shown us how. Even historically much independent evidence could be gathered if we really tried, not only by standard historical methods but by content analysis, by sensitivity to the "covert culture" as this may be unconsciously revealed in the very metaphors a writer uses,[38] and in related ways. Nor is it suggested that Amery was wrong in his facts as distinct from his interpretation of them. As it happens, an inquiry by Mark Abrams and Richard Rose provides some support for his opinion. In January–February, 1960, they undertook a small sample survey in fifty parliamentary constituencies selected at random.[39] Respondents were given a card listing fifteen personality traits, and in due course asked to say which four they thought "the most important for a good party leader." Not only did the trait "strong leader" head the list, but it was revealingly followed by "strong enough to make unwelcome decisions" (see Table 1).

So the danger of circularity can be averted in principle, although when we come to form particular judgments the "hard data" we need are often lacking. There is, in any case, the specific risk that the "nothing but" approach (i.e., of compressing the several factors [other than "the nature of the group"] "into" the political-culture factor) will mislead students into underestimating or even totally ignoring the *contributory* "causal" effect of those factors. We could ignore intermediate or subsidiary structures, including electoral procedures, only if each one was perfectly in tune with the political culture. The cautionary tale here is the parallel dispute about the relative "causal" force of (a) social structure as against (b) electoral procedures in bringing about (c) political-party configurations, or systems. As the American political sociologist Seymour Martin Lipset has remarked,[40] many social scientists, for the most part sociologists, tended to jump over (b) and lay a direct line from (a) to (c). But many political scientists not only clung stubbornly to the view that (b) has some "causal"

[37] *The Civic Culture* (Boston: Little, Brown and Company, 1965).
[38] Bernard Bowron, Leo Marx, and Arnold Rose, "Literature and Covert Culture," in *Studies in American Culture*, ed. Joseph J. Kwiat and Mary C. Turpie (Minneapolis: University of Minnesota Press, 1960).
[39] *Must Labor Lose?* (Harmondsworth, Eng.: Penguin Books Ltd., 1960).
[40] *The First New Nation* (London: Heinemann Educational Books Ltd., 1964), pp. 288–89.

Table 1

Traits	Views of:			
	All Respondents	Conservatives	Labour	Others
Strong leader	56%	59%	53%	53%
Strong enough to make unwelcome decisions	47%	49%	43%	50%

significance but also, as with Maurice Duverger in France,[41] produced evidence and argument in its support.

The debate cannot be summarized here, but the accession of Lipset himself in 1960 to the side of the political scientists probably marked the turning-point in it. The upshot is that electoral procedures are now given their "causal" due to an extent unheard of before Duverger took up his pen. As drawn by Lipset, the picture (given sufficient cases for analysis) now includes the following:

Electoral Procedures

Presidential system	plus	single-member districts and one plurality election	→	two-party system
Parliamentary system	plus	single-member districts and one plurality election	→	tendency toward two-party system
Parliamentary system	plus	single-member districts and alternative ballots or run-off (second) election	→	tendency to multi-party system
Parliamentary system	plus	proportional representation	→	multi-party system

True, these are "mere" correlations, to which we are not supposed in principle to attribute "causal" force, but Lipset himself had already referred to the "causal effect of electoral systems,"[42] which indeed is what in commonsense terms the debate had been all about.

What is the significance of this conclusion for our discussion? It means that students would be well advised not to conceive the important relationship as:

Political culture → party system

but, at the very least, as:

Political culture → electoral procedures → party systems (or configurations)
(i)   (ii)   (iii)

(Compare this with (a), (b), and (c) above.[43]) As applied to Britain, for example, it would be better for students *not* to "work back" directly from (iii) to (i), i.e.,

[41] *Political Parties,* 2nd English ed. (London: Methuen & Company Ltd., 1964).
[42] *The First New Nation,* p. 289, n. 4.   [43] P. 59.

from the modern two-party system to certain elements in the British political culture, namely, social deference and, above all, political pragmatism or disdain for doctrine. No doubt, as Harry Eckstein insisted,[44] that electoral system does "work in with" that political culture, but it does not follow, as students tend to infer, that no electoral system could "make a difference." On the contrary, suppose the two major political parties in Britain agreed to introduce proportional representation. That need not presuppose the slightest *general* change in British political culture; it *could* be done tomorrow by, in national terms, a handful of political leaders, either as part of a long-term strategy or even out of a sense of justice to, if not the Liberal party, then the persistent Liberal voters. Does anyone doubt that Britain would then *tend* to put on display a multi-party system? Since there would then be something of a discrepancy between (*i*) and (*ii*), the picture might be represented as:

Political culture	electoral procedures	party system
(i)	(ii)	(iii)

Between (*i*) and (*ii*) we expect congruence in the long run, in the absence of "friction." But at any given time they may diverge. Grant that and the possibility of the electoral system's making a causal contribution has also to be granted.

Of course, we must not swing over so far that we make too much of an electoral system. Joseph LaPalombara has pointed out, for example, that Italy had multi-parties before proportional representation was introduced for the first time in 1919.[45] If the *current* British electoral system were somehow introduced into Italy, no one supposes that a two-party system would result, or even that there would be much of a tendency toward it. In Italy the main "push" could be said to come either from the political culture or from the social structure, the electoral system being consequence rather than cause, although not lacking, presumably, a certain reinforcing effect in its own right. Accordingly, for Italy, we could jump from culture to party system if we wished.

What it comes down to, then, is that we would be wise at present to retain all the compound variables provisionally identified at the opening of our discussion, not compressing Variables 2, 3, and 4 into one variable, political culture, even though that would do for some systems. The truth is that each factor *may* contribute something in the causal sense, which means that the significance of any one may have to be judged *in terms* of one or more of the others. This is one of the valuable points in Eckstein's discussion.[46] In his later work especially, Duverger clearly distinguishes three sets of factors as shaping the character of the party system: socioeconomic (e.g, social classes); historical and cultural (e.g., religious divisions); and electoral (the procedures).[47] The last of these may

44 In Beer et al., *Patterns of Government*, pp. 134–35.

45 "The Italian Elections and the Problem of Representation," *American Political Science Review*, Vol. XLVII (September, 1953), p. 702.

46 See above, footnote 44.

47 *The Idea of Politics*, English ed. (London: Methuen & Company Ltd., 1966), p. 112.

be thought of as "aiding or hindering" the tendencies induced by the other two. This approach can be generalized, and so with Duverger's example to comfort us, we shall (until further notice) stick to our Variables 2, 3, 4, and 5, despite a certain awkwardness and a change in the level of abstraction.

IN THE LONG RUN

Let us now put more Time into our assessments, still keeping (at least to begin with) the same type of Actor (i.e., the business corporation) at the same level within the same two political systems. Merely to suggest a mode of analysis, we take two characteristic styles of action: (a) virtual co-option in government; (b) sustained public relations (PR) activity. The first will be set out in terms of similarities and differences and therefore of several variables, expressible in highly schematic form, suppressing some complications, as:

Variable 1 "plus" variables 2 and 4 $\longrightarrow$ virtual co-option in government

The second will be dealt with only "intrinsically," i.e., in terms of a group's inner tendencies, leaving the reader to "add" what variables he thinks fit in order to explain whatever inter-system differences he has observed.

Virtual Co-option in Government. In the mid-Fifties the executive departments in the United States were enmeshed in a web of about five to six thousand advisory committees. Some passed quickly out of sight; others survived but showed little signs of life. By no means all of these were of a kind to attract corporate representation, but we know that at the end of 1952, some 550 industry advisory committees had been attached to the National Production Authority, an agency of the Department of Commerce set up in 1950 after the outbreak of the Korean War.[48] A number of the important advisory committees brought the corporations right into the administrator's office. An outstanding example is afforded by the Business Council (formerly known as the Business Advisory Council), established in 1933 to advise the Department of Commerce. This body has been drawn from the biggest corporations in the land. By 1955 it could be officially said that the Council had brought in two of the four largest rubber companies, three of the five largest car manufacturers, three of the ten largest steel producers, four of the ten largest companies in chemicals, two of the three largest makers of electrical equipment, two of the three largest textile manufacturers, four of the sixteen largest oil companies, and three of the largest glass manufacturers.[49] The witnesses to this—the Celler Committee, a committee of the House—have to be designated hostile (to the Republican Administration), but their evidence, simply taken at its face value without the possible inferences

[48] Grant McConnell, *Private Power and American Democracy* (New York: Alfred A. Knopf, Inc., 1966), p. 264.
[49] *Ibid.*, p. 276.

from it, doubtless stands. Some smaller corporations have been represented certainly, but on the whole it is right to conclude that the Council has been staffed by "large corporate interests."[50] And "staffing" has in practice meant the major figures in the dominant corporations: board chairmen or presidents, commonly.[51]

Meanwhile, in late 1953, the residual functions of the National Production Authority had been inherited by the Business and Defense Services Administration (BDSA), the new Republican leadership virtually continuing a Democratic practice, arguably by then a tradition, of government–industry consultation. This had the effect of laying new trails from the corporations to the Department of Commerce. Thus three big corporations were to fill in turn the directorship of the Aluminum and Magnesium Division of BDSA; certain other corporations had the deputy directorship in their keeping. The Washington representative of a big paper manufacturing company became the Assistant Director of the Pulp, Paper, and Paperboard Division; the vice-president of a sales company linked to a large lumber producer became a Director of the Forest Products Division.[52]

All this represents, even for business, only the tip of the iceberg. Other corporations have been observed "homing" upon other Departments. The substantial oil companies, and not only the four major ones of the Business (Advisory) Council, man the National Petroleum Council, which, founded in 1946 as a continuation of a wartime body, hinges upon the Department of the Interior.[53] As with the Business Council, the corporations send their principals— presidents or board chairmen.

Beyond official co-option lies a kind of "functional equivalent"—*clientelism*. Two broad types may be distinguished, within and outside the "regular" Departments. The Cabinet Departments of Agriculture, Labor, and Commerce exemplify the former. Clientelism here means that one takes the vantage point of the Department as shepherd to its flock; for example, the Department of Agriculture may show too tender a concern for food producers (as against consumers).[54] Looked at from the other end of the telescope, and focusing upon Commerce as the Department that mainly concerns business corporations, clientelism may be presented as a procedure for ventured influence. Thus the corporations expect to influence the appointment of the Secretary of Commerce; they may even virtually appoint him.[55] Some Secretaries of Commerce, said to have enjoyed close links with corporations, seem to have been more responsive to them than to the President himself, e.g., Jesse Jones under Franklin Roosevelt.[56] There may also be first-order group influence upon appointments lower down the ladder, as in the special case of World War II, when the corporations rather than the trade associations provided the principal channel of recruitment to the

---

[50] Totton J. Anderson, "Pressure Groups and Intergovernmental Relations," *The Annals* (May 1965), p. 121.
[51] McConnell, *Private Power and American Democracy*, p. 276.
[52] *Ibid.*, p. 270.
[53] *Ibid.*, p. 272.
[54] Truman, *The Governmental Process*, p. 431.
[55] *Ibid.*, p. 403.
[56] *Ibid.*, p. 407. See Richard F. Fenno, "The Presidential Coalition: The Case of Jesse Jones," in *Readings in American Political Behavior*, ed. Raymond E. Wolfinger (Englewood Cliffs, N. J.: Prentice-Hall, Inc., 1966), Chapter Six.

federal service. Even in peacetime, and even within the "classified service" (recruited by merit), there is some coming and going between business and government service, conveying some possibilities of influence. It is perhaps significant, however, that we here slip into writing "business" rather than "corporation," for we begin to pass beyond the concept of a corporation's initiating and probing activities into one where corporate influence is far more inchoate. Nor should it ever be assumed that previous "social background" is destined automatically to be translated into current behavior;[57] that background has to be "balanced" against the strength, clarity, consistency, etc., of the norms of the Department into which the recruit comes (or, we could say, of his role, with its attendant sanctions). The proof of the pudding is in the eating; the question can be decided only empirically.

Corporations also busy themselves in a strange, though not unexplored, territory lying well outside the boundaries of the "regular" departments. Here stand the Commissions, characteristically charged with regulating (= supervising) some sphere of the economy—railroads, pipelines, and trucking; aviation; shipping; communications in the other sense, i.e., TV and radio; trade practices; tariffs; and power (in the sense of energy) are examples from a baker's dozen or so. These are the Commissions usually referred to as Independent Commissions. Not all are called "Commissions," however; e.g., Civil Aeronautics Board; not all have been judged independent in every sense. Constructed to be independent of, at least, the cabinet system and the President, the Commissions succeeded sufficiently, in 1937, to be characterized, officially but no doubt too sweepingly and dramatically, as "a headless fourth branch of the Government, responsible to no one. . . ." What concerns us here, however, is not the public-administration aspect as such but the common view that *some* of the Commissions have escaped the peril of "politics" only to fall victim to the interest-groups, some of which would be business corporations. One stock example is that of the railroads' influence upon the Interstate Commerce Commission, thanks to which the railroads are said to have benefited at the expense of the trucking companies. The Civil Aeronautics Board has also been criticized for discriminating in favor of establishing airlines, and of scheduled passenger lines as opposed to all-cargo lines in terms of rate structure.[58] It seems altogether likely that corporations have turned, and are turning, clientelism in this sense to their advantage (although if there are winners there must also be losers among them). As Mark Massel has written, the regulatory process is "a political function and not an exercise in technical jurisprudence."[59] And where politics is, there will the interest-groups be also. All in all, it may be that the *de facto* co-option which

[57] There are two incongruent traditions in the literature: (a) what a person brings to the policy-making role (i.e., his personality, or norms, from his prior socialization), and (b) the shaping power of the *current* role. The latter is fundamental to role theory, yet the behavior of businessmen "in and around" government is automatically assumed to be determined by their prior socialization. See Peter H. Rossi, "Community Decision-Making," in *Approaches to the Study of Politics*, ed. Roland Young (London: Stevens and Sons Ltd., 1958). Consider also J. P. Nettl, "Consensus or Elite Domination: The Case of Business," *Political Studies*, Vol. XIII (February, 1965).

[58] McConnell, *Private Power and American Democracy*, p. 286.

[59] Mark S. Massel, in *The Politics of Regulation*, ed. Samuel Krislov and Lloyd D. Musolf (Boston: Houghton Mifflin Company, 1964), p. 254.

is clientelism surpasses, in terms of interest-group significance, the official form of it.

In Britain, too, executive power is hedged about by systems of advice and consultation, there being perhaps some five hundred central advisory committees (a figure not comparable with the American). Business has a good share in this system, but it is attained much less by ties with the first-order (or operational) groups than with groups of the two higher orders. Certainly firms are often in touch with the Departments; and it is possible that some big firms have some autonomous influence (i.e., in their own right and not through a trade association). But the contrast with the United States is striking. How shall we explain these similarities and differences?

We saw that one component of "nature of the group," specialist or technical knowledge, was not readily usable in the short run (at least, not in the particular instance). But the longer the time period, the more versatile a component tends to be. Whatever their other limitations, the industrialists, builders, sellers of goods and services, know *what's what* and *how things work* in their own fields. At the same time—Variable 2—the persons (civil servants and politicians) comprising the Administration are, in the relevant respects, ignorant, partly as a result of foolish recruiting policies, partly unavoidably as the obverse of specialization. For whatever reason, their knowledge of the world of making and selling is limited. This would matter little if the worlds of government and business (= industry and commerce) did not overlap, but as they do, limited knowledge must be made up. Hence we observe in both systems a tendency to co-opt into government those whose knowledge is part of their working life.

As for the differences, if British *companies as such* are less incorporated into the system of government, it may be due partly to their being proportionately less important in terms of the adaptive (or economic) system. Compare, for instance, some industrial corporations in 1958. In the United States, each of the "top twenty" had sales of over $1,500 million; in Britain (in Europe even) that figure cut off three companies, two of which were partly Dutch.[60] Sixteen of those American corporations each had assets of more than $1,000 million, a "marker" bringing in two other companies in Britain (and two more in Europe.)[61] Using the test of numbers of persons, we find that, compared with Britain, about twice as many of these American companies employed 50,000 or more.[62] Of course, this comparison omits the British public corporations (nationalized industries) and is fraught with dangers, but counting in other corporations (e.g., in banking and insurance), the impression of corporate "giantism" in the United States does remain after the various qualifications have been made. Accordingly, we might expect more of the great corporations, *as such*, to be prominent in ventured influence than the great corporations, *as such*, in Britain. It is not surprising, for instance, to find that members of the Business (Advisory) Council were, up to the mid-1950's, also substantially drawn from these corporate giants,

---

[60] Royal Dutch/Shell; Unilever; British Petroleum. See *People, Power, and Politics,* ed. Lyman J. Gould and E. William Steel (New York: Random House, Inc., 1961), Chap. 24.

[61] Imperial Chemical Industries; British-American Tobacco; Philips (Netherlands); Fiat.

[62] The British companies are Royal Dutch/Shell; Unilever; Imperial Chemical Industries; British Motor Corporation (now British Leyland); Hawker Siddeley; Dunlop (rubber products); Guest, Keen and Nettlefords (engineering).

or that all three contenders for the aircraft contracts mentioned earlier (Western Electric, Boeing, and General Dynamics) were among the twenty largest industrial corporations in the United States. Alternatively, put Western Electric as a whole in another context, that of the British electrical engineering industry. After a great take-over battle in 1967, the General Electric Company (United Kingdom) (GEC) acquired Associated Electrical Industries (AEI). Even after the merger, the "league table" stood as shown in Table 2.

If "giantism" constitutes a "positive" reason for co-opting American business from the first-order level, Variable 4 may supply a "negative" reason, i.e., against representation only or mainly through national trade associations. The platitude has to be regularly repeated that, physically, Britain is only of the order severally of Kansas, Idaho, Minnesota, and Utah; is less considerable than Oregon and Wyoming; and is left far behind not only by Texas (naturally) but also by California, Colorado, Montana, Nevada, and New Mexico, without invoking Alaska. In Britain the size of the "social matrix" makes representation "for detail" through centralized trade associations workable and tolerable; in the United States that *alone* would be intolerable even if it worked.

These two variables "in confluence" explain, so to speak, corporate "strivings," but the "impact" depends upon certain components of Variable 2. The main difference to be accounted for here is constituted by that form of virtual co-option, clientelism. Clearly, the American system of public administration is far more "extended" and "loose-limbed" than the British. Even though the American Cabinet is no Cabinet in the British sense, the President obviously has to farm out his work, and the ten Cabinet Departments are something less than satellites to his sun. In his principal appointments to the Departments of Agriculture and of Labor as well as of Commerce he has to keep his eye on their respective clienteles, to which he may even have to defer; once appointed, the Cabinet heads may hunt with the hounds of the clientele rather than run with the President's hare. Even a subunit of the Army, apparently so firmly within the grasp of the President (both via the Defense Department and in his other role as Commander-in-Chief) has been able to practice an astonishing way-

Table 2

	Turnover (in millions of £)	Capital Employed (in millions of £)
1. General Electric, USA	7,239	3,492
2. General Telephone & Electric, USA	1,856	1,349
3. Western Electric, USA	1,205	709
4. Westinghouse Electric, USA	925	534
5. AEI/GEC—UK	445	—

Source: *The Times*, November 10, 1967.

wardness over the years, even in wartime.[63] This is the strange case of the Army Corps of Engineers insofar as it undertakes flood control, river and harbor works, and the like. If the Cabinet departments surrounding the President are not always very firmly under his control, how much more elusive are the thirteen or fourteen Independent Commissions, the eight public corporations (e.g., the Tennessee Valley Authority), and the score or more other agencies, such as the Federal Reserve System and the Veterans Administration.[64] Of course, the looseness of grip is not uniform. Many of the heads of the "other agencies" report directly to the President; some sit in the Cabinet. On the other hand, some heads have shown notable waywardness (or independence). What all this means, of course, is that a large part of the Administration is vulnerable to influence from the "outside," since the United States lacks (for good reason, in its own terms) a powerful civil service to make up for the President's loose hold on his administrative system. Variables 1 and 2 substantially explain why the "outside" that gets inside (at this point) should be, to a marked degree, the business corporation.

By contrast, the British system of public administration is far less permeable. It is far less fragmented, and its more unified structure is far better coordinated by the Cabinet than the American system permits. That alone tends to prevent *clientelism*, but a further defense is afforded by the character and recruitment of the civil service. The Ministry of Agriculture may be the exception that proves the rule, the wartime emergency having opened the gates to recruits from the farming industry to which, rather than the consumer, they remained devoted. But examples of such penetration by business firms are hard to come by. At the same time, ministers and civil servants operating a highly centralized, highly unified, system are only too delighted to deal not so much with firms as with representative bodies (themselves highly centralized) presumed to be speaking for the whole industry or trade.

Sustained PR Activity. Many secondary groups have to think of their relations with the public at large or their own particular public (or clientele), i.e., their *public relations*, and accordingly feel a "strain toward" the activity itself, defined in Britain (by the Institute of Public Relations) as "the deliberate, planned and sustained effort to establish and maintain mutual understanding between an organization and its public." Certainly the activity is not confined to business corporations or other business groups. Yet it seems to be characteristic of these in a sense that does not hold for other groups taken *as types*. Historically, it was American business corporations that felt their way toward the concept (as distinct from the words) *public relations*. It was an executive of an American railroad, for instance, who gave (1906) the landmark speech, "The Public Relations Problem of the Railroad." It was a president of the Bell Tele-

---

[63] Truman, *The Governmental Process*, p. 412. See also Arthur Maass, *Muddy Waters* (Cambridge, Mass.: Harvard University Press, 1951), and McConnell, *Private Power and American Democracy*, Chapter 7.

[64] In each case these were the principal units in the late Sixties. Ernest S. Griffiths, *The American System of Government*, 2nd rev. ed. (London: Methuen & Company Ltd., 1966), Chapter 9.

phone Company who was one of the first to define industry's public-relations problems and to think out their long-term adjustment,[65] i.e., to plan sustained PR activity. It was that company that launched (1908) national advertising of the prestige type, a species of PR. Meanwhile the legendary Ivy Lee had been practicing what others had been preaching: favorable "image-making" for the Pennsylvania Railroad which employed him as its director of publicity. Soon, as an independent professional, he was performing the same necessary service for Rockefeller's Standard Oil Company.[66] With Lee, of course, we pass beyond not only advertising but also "mere" press agentry to conveying "everything involved in the expression of an idea or an institution including the policy or the idea expressed." "The great publicity man," he pronounced, "is the man who advises his client what policy to pursue, which, if pursued, would create favorable publicity."[67]

From the beginning, such PR had obvious political implications but was still not quite political in the contemporary (or more specific) sense. That development may be dated for our purposes from the 1930's, when under the shock of unprecedented economic depression and the concomitant public criticism of business, "many" corporations extended their staff (as in "line and staff") to include vice-presidents for PR.[68] In particular, of course, the "New Deal," the political response to the depression, included the National Industrial Recovery Act (NIRA) of 1933, which directly encouraged trade unionism by guaranteeing collective bargaining. Within two years NIRA had been undermined by a Supreme Court decision, but its labor provisions rose Phoenix-like from the ashes as the National Labor Relations (or Wagner) Act, accompanied by a permanent board invested with powers for the enforcement of those provisions. Surviving a challenge through the courts, this Act still ranks as labor's greatest legislative achievement. No wonder that after the 1936 election, which gave President Roosevelt a second term, leaders of such firms as General Motors, General Foods, United States Steel, and the American Telephone and Telegraph (among others) declared PR to be "Industry's Number One Problem."[69]

A problem defined so extensively was likely to be tackled on the widest basis, i.e., by a "peak," and so it proved, the main burden being borne by the National Association of Manufacturers (NAM), whose president at the time was associated with the characterization just quoted. Since the early years of the century the NAM had played a very active anti-union role, not without some success, but it could not stem the New Deal tide. Failing to recover ground through the courts, it worked out in 1936 a long-term PR strategy that in time included: a regular news service to weekly and other newspapers; a cartoon series that became celebrated ("Uncle Abner Says"); newspaper advertisements; a bulletin for foremen; material for factory magazines and also for putting into

---

[65] Norton E. Long, quoted in Harwood L. Childs, *Public Opinion: Nature, Formation, and Role* (Princeton, N. J.: D. Van Nostrand Co., Inc., 1965), p. 274.

[66] *Ibid.*, p. 275.

[67] Quoted in Stanley Kelley, Jr., *Professional Public Relations and Political Power* (Baltimore: The Johns Hopkins Press, 1956), p. 18.

[68] Childs, *Public Opinion*, p. 277.

[69] *Ibid.*, p. 278.

pay envelopes; and posters, speeches, and films on the private-enterprise theme. Eventually, in propitious circumstances after the Second World War, the work of a decade culminated in "a volume of publicity and pressure seldom equaled"[70] for the purpose of amending the Wagner Act—large-scale broadcasts; newspaper advertisements said to have reached forty million readers; material distributed to 7,500 weekly papers; "Industry's Views" to 2,500 columnists and editorial writers; special bulletins for special groups, such as teachers, women's clubs, and clergymen; even special pamphlets for use in schools. The upshot (not necessarily cause and effect, of course) was the Labor–Management Relations Act of 1947, better known as the Taft–Hartley Act, passed over the President's veto.

British firms reached their "New Deal" crisis after 1945, when the advent of the first Labour government with an overall majority put them out of countenance and threatened, through the policy of nationalization, to put some of them out of business. As victims perversely unwilling to lay their heads upon the block, the steel companies are the type-case, putting up a long and stubborn resistance, in which PR was fundamental. They ran a campaign before the 1950 election, but Labour was returned, if with a tiny majority, and the industry was taken into public ownership, only to be taken out again after the Conservatives came back into office in October, 1951. By 1957 not only the steel firms but many others felt positively threatened as Labour's stock rose in the aftermath of the Suez episode and as Labour committed itself to extensions of public control. Hence, in 1958 some two hundred companies in all, in light engineering and machine tools as well as in steel, paid for a vast poll of public opinion in marginal constituencies in order to elicit attitudes to nationalization.[71] The bill for this, the controversial Colin Hurry survey, came to about £475,000. One important steel firm, Stewart and Lloyds, not only paid part of that but also ran its own advertising campaign at a cost of some £269,000. The British Iron and Steel Federation (the trade association) also fought the good fight through an advertising campaign, at an estimated cost of some £287,000.

Once again, the Conservative success in the 1959 election saved the steelmasters' bacon. But by the early Sixties anxiety was again gnawing at some Federation vitals, and in late 1963–early 1964 another advertising campaign was under way. This, daringly continued almost to the eve of the election in October, 1964 (i.e., risking infraction of the law on electoral expenditure), cost perhaps £650,000, about two-and-a-quarter times the Federation spending before the 1959 election. That, raised by a levy on the corporate members, was perhaps a measure of the Federation's desperation in 1963–64. Meanwhile, Stewart and Lloyds had returned to the fray on their own account, spending possibly £203,000. The United Steel Company weighed in with its own series of advertisements, which may have run up a bill of £100,000. The Steel Company of Wales and Dorman Long each devoted little less to the same purpose. Five other

---

[70] Robert E. Lane, James D. Barber, and Fred I. Greenstein, *An Introduction to Political Analysis*, 3rd ed. (Englewood Cliffs, N. J.: Prentice-Hall, Inc., 1962), pp. 94–95.

[71] D. E. Butler and Richard Rose, *The British General Election of 1959* (London: Macmillan & Co. Ltd., 1960), p. 244.

companies played their part, bringing the total (including Stewart and Lloyds' and United Steel's) to about £640,000, not much short of the Federation's level. So the grand total was a staggering £1,298,000.[72]

The long rearguard action of the steel companies (as it appears in retrospect) was only the most protracted of the post-1945 campaigns undertaken by firms. Of the shorter campaigns, Tate and Lyle's in 1949–50 to ward off the nationalization of its sugar refining business was the most memorable. Its PR advisers, Aims of Industry Limited, thought of everything, including the drawing on the sugar packet itself of a "little man" in the shape of a sugar cube. "Mr. Cube" and his messages were thus carried into every home in the shopping basket.[73] In the event, the Labour party only just clung to office, and did not proceed with the proposal, although whether as cause and effect, only heaven knows.

Although our intention was to confine ourselves to the first-order level, we have been able to do so in neither the American nor the British case. In Britain, the Iron and Steel Federation, we saw, fought shoulder to shoulder with the steel companies. Under the same sword of Damocles, the road hauliers (or truckers) tried through the Road Haulage Association (RHA) to avoid the unkind cut, fighting in the first part of 1947 in close liaison with the Opposition. They lost that battle if not the war, being denationalized after the Conservative Opposition was again converted into the Government. However, if a longer time perspective is taken, the apparent war has to be reclassified as an episodic battle. By 1959, in the wake of a Labour party proposal to renationalize, the RHA was again running a small PR campaign, costing some £39,000. Labour, however, was not returned, and by the 1964 election had fallen silent on the subject, so that the RHA's PR output then was confined to a mere pamphlet. But just nine years after the "spring offensive" of 1959, the RHA again entered the lists in opposition to a new Transport Bill that, although not a nationalizing measure, was intended to favor railroad traffic at the expense of the truckers. Working in, as before, with the Conservative Opposition, and guided by a PR professional, the RHA used "teach-ins" for unraveling the 169 clauses and 18 schedules of the bill; mounted "freedom rallies"; and distributed posters, leaflets, and stickers (such as this—seen on a delivery van—"Keep Transport Free: Defeat the Transport Bill").

These were fundamentally "crisis" campaigns, that is, designed to meet particular contingencies. Taking part in them but also making a long-term effort were two other bodies, the Economic League and Aims of Industry Limited, both essentially anchored in first-order economic groups. The former was founded in 1919, that year of revolutionary shock-waves in Europe; it is meant to be a bulwark for "personal freedom and free enterprise." It seems to be mainly the "free enterprisers" who dip their hands in their pockets to keep the organization going. Apparently they are not ungenerous: in 1964 the Director-General confessed to "a *steady* annual expenditure of about £250,000."[74] The League sends

---

[72] Richard Rose, *Influencing Voters* (London: Faber & Faber Ltd., 1967), p. 130.
[73] H. H. Wilson, "Techniques of Pressure," *Public Opinion Quarterly*, Vol. XV, No. 2 (Summer, 1951), pp. 225–42.
[74] *Sunday Times*, June 14, 1964. Emphasis added.

press releases to the newspapers, but has relied mainly upon the appeal of words spoken at the factory gate, though with leaflets to remember them by.

Aims of Industry Limited was fathered in 1942 by an executive of a firm of spark-plug manufacturers, but developed from 1946 onwards by some very rich uncles, Rolls Royce, Ford's, Imperial Chemical Industries, Tate and Lyle, Handley Page, Associated Electrical Industries, and English Electric among them. It has long claimed the support of no fewer than 4,000 companies and trade and industrial organizations, which in the mid-Sixties were subscribing something like £100,000 a year for the more or less "routine" PR work. Such subscriptions were conveniently tax-deductible. Like the League, Aims has ventured into the streets and taken a stand outside the factory gates, but has to a far greater extent resorted to traditional PR through the press and BBC. Editorial material has been syndicated each week to about 900 newspapers and magazines: this has included four feature articles supplemented by background comment for leader (or editorial) writers; news stories on free-enterprise themes; a London Letter; a gossip column for women; a feature for young readers. Every two weeks an Overseas London Letter has gone to some 400 newspapers throughout the world. On that ample foundation, Aims in the later Fifties was able to claim 150,000 column-inches in one year, putting in the shade the Economic League's 36,000 column-inches.[75]

An organization so poised can of course be readily summoned to meet major political emergencies. With the "Mr. Cube" campaign in 1949–50, it made a highly successful political debut. It then reverted to its more general PR role, but when in the later Fifties a keener political wind again blew, Aims offered some counters to nationalization, supplying literature for putting into pay packets (an old NAM device), pamphlets, and booklets. This, on the most informed view,[76] does not rank as a separate campaign, but reaching a climax before the 1959 election and costing perhaps £107,000, it is not to be sneezed at. The first campaign proper since the early Fifties was mounted in 1964. Press releases and 600,000 leaflets were distributed, but the principal component was a national advertising campaign mainly directed at the electorate as a whole. This took the form to a small extent of posters but was largely press advertising in which the central theme was "Say No to Nationalization," matched by a thumbs-down motif, a neat "knocking" response to the Labour party's "Let's Go with Labour" and its supporting thumbs-up.[77] The total bill came to about £270,000,[78] of which some £20,000 was spent on press advertising in the few weeks before the date of the election was announced.

Now the wheel has turned full circle, for we are back to something like a "crisis" campaign. A second-order group that has quietly undertaken a long-term PR campaign not dependent upon particular exigencies is the British

---

[75] *Scope*, September, 1959, p. 33.

[76] Rose, *Influencing Voters*, p. 100. For the facts, see Butler and Rose, *The British General Election of 1959*, pp. 248 and 252.

[77] Richard Rose, in D. E. Butler and Anthony King, *The British General Election of 1964* (London: Macmillan & Co. Ltd., 1965), pp. 370–71.

[78] Rose, *Influencing Voters*, p. 106. This total is a little above the one Rose had reported in his appendix to Butler and King, *ibid.*, p. 375, Aims having at the time inadvertently omitted the cost of a small poster campaign.

Trawlers' Federation (Distant Water Section). Even in the 1920's it experimented with a small advertising campaign, but in the early 1950's it embarked on full-scale PR with the aid of outside specialist firms. In addition to institutional advertisements, it placed human-interest stories in the press and even sought the ear of the *party* committees in the House of Commons.[79]

At the same level, or tier, in the United States there is so much to report that only a book could do it justice. Suffice to say that it ranges from the long-term PR program, hardly ever innocent of political implications, of the Association of American Railroads, to that of the American Petroleum Institute and its one-time offshoot, the Oil Industry Information Committee, which could not have been fairly accused of political innocence either. With its quite different stance, the Committee for Economic Development (CED) (1942) has also to be reckoned with (in the post-1945 period) as apparently anchored in some firms and undertaking a PR role, if of an unusually "reasoned" kind. Higher up stand not only the NAM but also the U.S. Chamber of Commerce, with its press releases and its considerable journal, *The Nation's Business*. Make an allowance for our far more considerable ignorance and it is plain that the total PR effort is both prodigious and staggeringly expensive.

It is true as well as plain that we have now strayed far beyond the first-order level. But *not* to have done so would have been wholly unrealistic because all or almost all the higher-order groups mentioned are (or were) anchored in business corporations at the first-order level. Put together, they can be seen as all of a piece, the corporations forming the foundation, structural and financial. To say that is not to resurrect a version of the business-conspiracy thesis. Even a one-eyed observer can make out that business is simply not monolithic. What is suggested is that PR is characteristic of the business corporation and its "emanations" in a sense that is not true of any other *type* of group. Do not take that for granted: see if you can match the PR activity of the business groups *qua* groups. I think that our observations are at least congruent with our expectations (page 50). The point, then, is: different groups, different endowments, tendencies toward different styles of action.

---

[79] Morris Davis, "British Public Relations: A Political Case Study" *Journal of Politics*, Vol. 24, No. 1 (1962).

CHAPTER FIVE

THE INFLUENCE OF INTEREST-GROUPS

Can we compare the actual influence of interest-groups and in broad terms account for the differences? The tentative nature of that question is justifiable, for this is a real Irish bog of a subject that has claimed many victims, not all of them innocent. It is useless to pretend that in the present state of our knowledge we can have an empirically well-grounded discussion; even our conceptual grasp of *influence* (as of its ugly sister, *power*) is far from secure. However, we can reach some relatively firm ground where we may stand, if not without trepidation, to survey the scene.

WHAT IS INFLUENCE?

For the purposes of this book, we first take the (reconstructed) vantage point of Actor, and then move in the direction of what used to be thought of as real definition. That is, while we cannot ignore the traditional meanings given to *influence, power,* and *authority* (to mention only a close family circle of concepts), we ought to set out from the specific relationship under scrutiny, and only later allow ourselves the luxury of worrying about a name for it. That relationship, of course, is:

$$PA \longrightarrow T : G$$

But now we focus upon the extent to which the Goal (reflecting the group's claim) is "converted" into the required decision, so the code might be put as:

$$PA \longrightarrow T : D (= Decision)$$

Obviously, this "output," *D*, may fall far short of the "input" of ventured influence, but let us start from the simple case where *PA* gets substantially what it asked for. The latent ambiguity of the arrowed relationships now thrusts itself to the surface. Does the arrow indicate: (a) "mere" transmission, leaving open the possibility that *T* might have reached that very decision even if no representations had been made; or (b) that *T* acted against the grain, i.e., would not have so acted had it not been for the impact of *PA* upon it?

I do not think there can be any doubt that the arrow must be taken to indicate the second relationship. In saying this there need be no appeal to intuition; we need only recall the politicosociological history of the concept: the situations in which it was invented and developed and the concrete relationships it has always designated. Above all, we take the vantage point of the Actor, whom we must presume to define the situation as requiring *T* to act more or less against the grain. If that is agreed, an immediate link-up with other branches of political science and with other social sciences becomes possible. For political science Robert Dahl may be summoned to bear witness: "A has power over B to the extent that he can get B to do something that B would not otherwise do."[1] Social psychologist Dorwin Cartwright is in the same broad current with his notion of O's ability to induce a behavioral or psychological change in P as indicative of the range of O's power.[2] Or turn to the English historian R. H. Tawney: power is "the capacity of an individual, or group of individuals, to modify the conduct of other individuals or groups in the manner which he desires, and to prevent his own being modified in the manner in which he does not."[3] The last part of this quotation (from "to modify . . .") has, it seems, the overtones of Dahl's "something that B would not otherwise do." Many other writers could be cited.

As against this, however, a note of dissent has been struck by the American political scientist Martha Derthick, attacking Dahl's formulation with specific reference to interest-group studies:

> A fundamental difficulty is that of proving that B would not have done what A wanted him to do even in the absence of A's efforts to exert power. Although we can discover that A wanted B to take a certain action, and we can observe that A has certain resources of potential power and used the available means to bring them to bear on B, and we can observe that B took the action that A intended, we still cannot be sure that B would not have taken the action without A's efforts. At least we would have great difficulty in estimating a probability that A's action affected B, which is what Dahl's conceptual scheme requires if we are to judge the amount of A's power.[4]

This is a difficulty, and it is fundamental. Derthick's own suggestion, however, is bold rather than workable. So far as the concept of power is concerned,

---

[1] "The Concept of Power," in *Introductory Readings in Political Behavior*, ed. S. Sidney Ulmer (Chicago: Rand McNally & Co., 1961), p. 344.
[2] *Studies in Social Power* (Ann Arbor: University of Michigan, 1959), pp. 208–9.
[3] *Equality* (London: George Allen & Unwin Ltd., 1931), p. 229.
[4] *The National Guard in Politics* (Cambridge, Mass.: Harvard University Press, 1965), p. 7.

she would have us "forget about" the Actor–Target connection altogether, the better to concentrate upon the Actor–Achievement connection:

> A group's power is the ratio of its achievements to its goals. Power is at a maximum when achievements and goals are in balance.

This is neat but scarcely convincing. In the first place, Derthick appeals to intuition, common sense, and usage: when an Actor is said to be "powerful" do we not mean he "gets what he wants"? But there "gets" is surely ambiguous: it hardly implies "without lifting a finger." On the contrary, I believe, "gets" implies effort, exertion. Certainly it would fly in the face of all usage to dub the decision or policy an "achievement" if this were not in some substantial sense attributable to Actor, whereas for Derthick:

> To establish that a group "has power," it is not necessary to judge the extent to which the actions are responses to activities of the group in pursuance of [the group's] claims.

That would no doubt simplify research: all we should have to do is to list an interest-group's goals (claims), sit back and be patient, ticking off the corresponding but inconsequential decisions as the golden years passed by. Second, the actual use of the concept would yield odd results. A tiny interest-group whose single claim in, say, five years was somehow matched by a suitable Target-decision sometime would eventually rank in the pantheon with a big group whose dozen claims in the same period were somehow matched then by a dozen suitable Target-decisions. And if the "matching" decisions were "only" six, the big group would have to be accounted an under-achiever compared with the smaller group. Thus Martha Derthick's remedy seems worse than the disease. I think we have to learn to live with our affliction, keeping it under reasonable control, since it does not actually keep us from going about our business in the other parts of the field, not even within the subdivision that forms the subject of this book. The truth is that the Actor–Target connection is "built into" the interest-group concept, both historically and by the very fact of Observer's taking the perspective of the Actor. We cannot discard it without destroying the concept as a whole. What we should discard is the expectation that every dimension of a concept is going to prove useful in every respect when we venture forth into practical applications.

Reverting, then, to the main line, now free of obstruction, we have a concept for which we require a name. The principal candidates are "power" (as already encountered) and "influence." The attribution of "power" is certainly possible. On the other hand, the link might cause some confusion because, according to a long Anglo-American tradition,[5] "power" conveys the capacity to exact very severe penalties for infractions of the law and other social norms.

---

[5] "Political power, then, I take to be a right of making laws with penalties of death, and consequently all less penalties, for the regulating and preserving of property, and of employing the force of the community, in the execution of such laws, and in defense of the commonwealth from foreign injury; and all this only for the public good." — John Locke.

Such penalties have been confined to the state, or government, which is alone entitled to use (as John Locke put it) "the force of the community." It is in keeping with this tradition that Lasswell and Kaplan wish to treat power as a special case of the exercise of influence, which "consists in affecting the policies of others than the self," a policy being a projected goal. "It is the threat of sanctions which differentiates power from influence in general."[6] Thus "influence" is put forth to denote "our" concept.

The authorities, then, do not speak with a single voice. For us here the outcome of the argument is a matter of indifference, since the important thing is to identify the relevant relationship (and so, according to one tradition, to "really define" it). Having done so, we could stipulate either "power" or "influence" and have a ready-made defense, but I long ago[7] chose "influence" for a discussion of some interest-groups, and persist in that choice now because it is consistent with Robert Dahl's usage in his volume in this series. Following Lasswell and Kaplan, Dahl in this later work of his equates *power* with *coercive influence* and "hooks" it on specifically to the state.[8] This usage leaves the way open for *influence* as that *"relation among actors in which one actor induces other actors to act in some way they would not otherwise act."*[9]

MEASURES OF INFLUENCE

We now have the concept and its name and are ready to ask: How can we measure it? This is where we need a sure-footed guide with a large lantern to see us through the treacherous bog. If at all possible, call upon the services of Robert Dahl, Chapter Three of his volume in this series, before proceeding further. Bending his analysis to our purpose, we proceed from the notion, inherent in the concept of interest-group,[10] of influence as *PA*'s inducing *T* to do something that *T* would not otherwise have done. This at once suggests three conceivable measures of influence:

    I. How many *T*'s can *PA* influence?
    II. How far did any particular *T* have to move, or change?
    III. What did the move, or change, "cost" any particular *T*, psychologically speaking?

All three measures presuppose a given issue, or range (or scope) of Target-decision.

Cases I and II may be illustrated by adapting Dahl's own example. Take our usual code (*PA* $\longrightarrow$ *T* : *G*), and let it be used for two individual Actors,

---

[6] Harold D. Lasswell and Abraham Kaplan, *Power and Society* (London: Routledge & Kegan Paul Ltd., 1952), pp. 71 and 76. But by "sanctions" these writers, just like modern role theorists in sociology, invariably include rewards as well as punishments.

[7] *The Politics of Influence.*

[8] *Modern Political Analysis*, 2nd ed., a companion volume in this series. In his 1957 article (see note 1, above), Dahl had used "power" but left open the issue of terminology.

[9] *Ibid.*

[10] Dahl derives his first three measures of influence partly, by analogy, from the concept of force in mechanics. My source, on the other hand, is the interest-group concept itself.

treating *T* at the pre-decisional stage where it may well be conceived not as a whole but as its individual members. Then look at Figure 6. We deal here with a single issue: the raising of teachers' salaries. Green and Thompson, the Private (for illustration, individual) Actors, are out to influence the *T*, the School Board, effectively "reduced" to three members, A, B, and C.[11] The asterisks indicate the initial increases that A, B, and C are prepared to make. Now Thompson cannot do anything with A or C (hence the deletion marks in the diagram), although he can persuade B to switch from $250 to $500 (see dotted line). On the other hand, Green is able not only to match that,[12] but also to persuade A to go all the way from a nil increase to $500. In these circumstances, we might say that Green is more influential than Thompson in two senses, in being able:

I. To move *more* (members of) Targets, A and B as against only B (on C, of course, Green and Thompson cancel out)
II. To get A to move "so far"[13]

Case II leads on naturally to Case III. Look back at Fig. 6. B is willing to shift ground to the extent of $250 only. But suppose B is from Vermont (or Aberdeen in Scotland, or Cardiganshire in Wales), where, it is alleged, people do not readily part with as much as a penny: might not B's pain and sacrifice

[11] In the original example there was a fourth Target-individual, D. He is given a rest here because he, Green, and Thompson agree on an increase of $1,000, which, however, they cannot get accepted.

[12] Is there, then, a further problem here of who "really" moves B?

[13] If you did look up Dahl's discussion, be warned that I have kept to the detail to avoid confusing you but have economized space by using one illustration to indicate two measures at once. Thus my I = Dahl's case 5. My Case II would be more clearly exemplified by attributing to Thompson the ability to move A to, say, $250, or any positive "distance" less than Green can bring about.

Figure 6

SINGLE ISSUE (OR SCOPE)

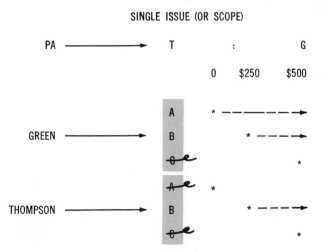

exceed A's? If so, B's true "distance" would be the greater. Here we ought to take into the reckoning the cost of the "move" in a sense reminiscent of one of the very early senses of *cost* in economic theory: the pain of giving something up. Alternatively, this might be expressed as *strength of normative commitment*.

Here, in principle, are three conceivable measures of interest-group influence. In practice, of course, we usually lack the crucial information. But if we look, we may find—*something*. By thinking along these lines we are at least sensitized to items that have to be allowed for in the balance sheet by the exercise of judgment. Thus, in weighing up the achievement of General Dynamics,[14] we are prompted to make some allowance for the fact that the Defense Department had been officially recommended to award the contract to the Boeing Company. Moreover, the attempt to produce measures of influence has the effect of warning us off certain sorts of comparisons as extremely hazardous, and so of giving shape to, and saving us from avoidable error in, other parts of the analysis, as, for instance, in the discussion of styles of action. Thus there may well be uncovenanted benefits beyond our immediate vision. This is outstandingly true of another possible measure of influence not yet discussed: Case IV.

Imagine some peak trade association and peak trade union within the same political system. The range, or scope, of the (public) decisions that they seek to influence is obviously far from being identical. Suppose we could show that (in, say, the United States) the trade association has had more influence than the trade union over tariff policy, but that the trade union has had more influence than the trade association over immigration policy. Supposing further that these were the only issues, which of the groups should be accounted the more influential? Obviously we cannot begin to answer that unless we know the relative importance of the two scopes, i.e., of tariff policy and of immigration policy. This is analogous to Robert Dahl's formulation: How *can* we compare Jack Dempsey and Babe Ruth as athletes? We can compare Dempsey to the French boxer Georges Carpentier, whom he knocked out, and to his fellow-American boxer Gene Tunney, by whom he was in turn defeated. Even then some imponderables remain: Dempsey had a far longer reign as champion, but Tunney's much shorter one was by design—he planned to get in and out of the ring fast, as soon as he had "made it." But boxing and baseball are incomparable *unless* we can agree about their order of importance.

If we cannot compare Dempsey and Ruth as athletes because there is no common ground, are we able to discover some? Suppose Dempsey's name were to be found on that plaque of famous names at Yankee Stadium,[15] that Ruth rivaled him in the ring, but that Dempsey were a far better golfer. In ordinary conversation we would probably agree to the proposition that Dempsey, with two "about equals" and one "plus," was the better athlete. Similarly, can we not agree to say that if (over a period) a certain peak trade association is (a) *about as* influential as a certain union peak in respect of the use of injunctions

---

[14] See above, p. 53.

[15] Before he played for the Yankees, Ruth turned out for the Boston Red Sox, whose fortunes might conceivably be somewhat improved if he were to be reincarnated at Fenway Park.

in labor disputes and in open-shop policy, but (*b*) *more* influential in tariff policy and administration, then it is the more influential *over the total range*? I myself would go further. If in "real life" it were possible to relate more than three items, assembling more "pluses" for the trade association, I would be prepared to take a "minus" into account and still strike a balance. Suppose we added in: (*c*) *less* influential in respect of immigration policy. Given some more "pluses" for the trade association, I would still be willing to judge it the more influential *over the whole range*. Of course, this would be a very crude conversation-piece assessment rather than a scientific one, but we have to adopt something like it *if* a judgment is required of us, as it often is, for public life demands judgments (and decisions) even when the material for these is obscure and recalcitrant.

So we emerge from the bog bearing four possible measures of interest-group influence:

    I. How many Targets can this interest-group influence?
    II. To what extent did the particular Target have to change ground under the interest-group's impulsion?
    III. What did the change at II cost the Target in terms of normative commitment?
    IV. Over how many scopes (*or*, over what total range) can an interest-group operate?

Defective as we know these measures to be in practice, we may yet gain some illumination if we approach any particular problem (in public life or academic research) armed, as Robert Dahl remarks, with "several, perhaps all, of the kinds of measures we have examined."[16] No doubt answers to II and III will usually be elusive; but to I and IV, perhaps less so. Notice, however, that in some political systems I and IV will severally yield something resembling the same answer, depending upon the degree of Target-specialization, territorial as well as functional. The United States, for example, furnishes interest-groups with many more autonomous Targets than does France or Britain, where interest-groups, however wide-ranging (in terms of scope), converge upon a smaller number of autonomous Targets, notably, of course, upon the Administration. In such systems, question I will obviously be unfruitful. Even in systems more generously endowed, in fact, it is likely to be useful only as a supplementary "weighting" factor. In this sense, IV (for what it's worth) is the more nearly universal indicator.

OPERATIONAL PROCEDURES

Consciously courting error, but by the same token allowing for it, we may take one step further along the road toward valid comparisons[17] if we draw out from the discussion so far some of the implicit "operational" procedures. We shall err on the safe side if we: (a) compare only groups located at the same level, where

---

[16] *Modern Political Analysis*, 2nd edition.
[17] These considerations also shape the discussion of styles of action. See above, pp. 48–72.

"distance" between scopes can be expected to be smaller than with groups located at different levels; (b) given the level, compare only those groups "homing" on the same Target. Here again the rationale is that insofar as legislatures and, say, government departments have characteristic decision-making ranges, their separation as Targets will do something to make comparisons less inadequate in terms of scope. Not that scope is the only consideration. Although normally we cannot calculate changes of "Target-commitment," we have to be aware of the imponderables. Confining ourselves to one type of Target might reduce error in a particular assessment.

What this comes to is that, within a given political system, we would *not* compare a corporation and a national trade union, for in my "functionalist" schema they occupy different positions in social space. This is not simply a metaphor, for it seems very likely that the scope of the influence of first- and second-order groups will vary beyond the permissible limit for comparison. On the other hand, comparing a national trade union with a national trade association (two second-order groups) may keep us within the permissible limit. Second, taking these two second-order groups, we would *not* relate the trade association's influence with a government department (over a certain scope) to the trade union's influence (over a certain scope) with the legislature, but stick rather to the influence of each upon, say, the legislature (over some total scope, and within a certain period). With intersystem comparisons, the danger of error tends to increase alarmingly, especially on account of "scope-incomparability." Here we would be wise to observe yet another self-denying ordinance, restricting ourselves to the same type of Actor as well as the same level and the same type of Target. That restriction was anticipated in our comparative sketch of the aircraft companies' campaigns in the United States and Britain, and in the interrelated discussion of styles of action. For intrasystem comparisons, one procedure (which we may label A) might be as follows:

1. Select some instances of "issue-convergence" involving two or three major Actors in opposition to each other over a period of time
2. Establish and date the nature of their initial claims and the subsequent "internal" development of these
3. Judge the initial position of the (autonomous) Target (from official documents; official and semi-official pronouncements; reports in interest-group files and journals of Target's views expressed in correspondence, at meetings, etc.; interviews with Actors and Target-members; and so on)
4. Chart what the several Actors did in pursuit of their claims
5. Examine the policy or decision reached by Target, compare it with item 3, and judge how far the policy was a consequence of item 4[18]

---

[18] Obviously, this is a "mixed" procedure, drawing upon some of the methods of the historian as well as of the behavioral scientist (insofar as the latter interviews Actors and Targets to determine views and meanings). This is inevitable in some sections of our work. As I have written elsewhere: "one is driven into making tentative judgments about the effectiveness of influence that have more in common with the historian's craft than the political 'scientist's.' " (*The Politics of Influence*, p. 232.) This drew from the famous historian A. J. P. Taylor the comment in a review: "quite a smack in the eye for us poor historians." ("Old Bill Goes into Politics," *Observer*, May 5, 1963.) I did not mean to disparage the

For example, in the United States, one might, for item 1, examine that cluster of controversial issues: union shop, closed shop,[19] and "right to work." Over the years, these have consistently engaged major Actors in strong, even bitter, opposition to each other, e.g., the National Metal Trades Association; the National Association of Manufacturers and its offshoots;[20] the AFL, CIO, and of course AFL-CIO. Some three-quarters-of-a-century of move and countermove reached a kind of climax after World War II in the Taft–Hartley Act (1947), which outlawed the closed shop and made the union shop legal only after an affirmative vote by a majority of employees. Yet the issue has not quite faded away: an important amendment in 1951 tipped the scales toward AFL-CIO, and the running fight has been continued at the level of the states in terms of "right-to-work" legislation. Since such legislation has been enacted by some 40 per cent of the states, it looks as if AFL-CIO has suffered continuing setbacks. But what is the industrial significance of such states? If they are predominantly agricultural, AFL-CIO's influence might yet be much greater than it seems on the surface. And in (estimated) fact perhaps two collective-bargaining contracts out of three in the whole USA have a union-shop provision. That looks like real influence, but then we have to take into account the Labor–Management Reporting and Disclosure Act (Landrum–Griffin) of 1959. In any event, there is material here for several studies usefully bearing upon comparisons of influence within a certain scope over time.

Another instance of "issue-convergence" engaging major Actors comes from the same area of social space: the use of injunctions in labor disputes. This question could be charted over much the same period as for the open-shop issue, but particularly from 1914, when the Clayton Act seemed to herald a new dawn for the AFL in this respect as in some others. In fact, it soon proved to be a false dawn, and the work had to be done all over again in the Norris–La Guardia Act of 1932. But in 1947 the courts decided that this Act did not apply to the U.S. government *qua* employer. Turning to other systems, we might examine with profit the course of the peculiarly German movement for workers' participation in management and for co-determination from, say, 1920 to 1951, when success came to the unions despite the federal government and despite various employers' associations that had set up a great fighting fund for a PR campaign to "stop the rot." A re-examination of the "explosion of 1936"[21] in France (the spontaneous strikes and occupation of factories) and the Matignon Agreement that followed might be instructive from the point of view of comparisons of influence. Here there would be complications. The nominal line-up was the employers' Confédération Générale de la Production Française v. the main union "peak," the Confédération Générale du Travail, allied with some others but with the Christian "peak," Confédération Française des Travailleurs Chrétiens, excluded. That, however, was not the "real" line-up, because the

---

historian's craft, only to stress *informed judgment* as opposed to *verification*. In general, I am strongly in favor of political scientists' reading far more history than they evidently do.

[19] A shop is *closed* when you can't get in without a union card; *union*, when you can't stay in without one.

[20] See Harmon Zeigler, *Interest Groups in American Society* (Englewood Cliffs, N. J.: Prentice-Hall Inc., 1965), pp. 112–13.

[21] Jean-Daniel Reynaud, *Les Syndicats en France* (Paris: Armand Colin, 1963), p. 87.

government itself played a crucial role. But that should make the study more interesting. So one could go on. There are probably many instances of issue-convergence available for reconstruction in terms of comparative influence, some of which might enable researchers to identify the Target's ostensible initial position with tolerable (in)accuracy. Even those who warm only to contemporary analyses will not lack material; what was lacking for too long was a clarification of the concept of influence, and a clear warning not only of the more obvious dangers but also of the subtler ambiguities in all comparative assessments.

Another possible procedure (which we label B) is the collection and "addition" of scopes within which interest-groups, preferably by Procedure A, are judged to be influential. Here again, the material has hardly been worked up in a form suitable for borrowing. It seems likely that some judgments in the literature, e.g., about the influence of "business" (usually left undefined), do rest upon some such "summation" of the scopes within which business is thought, or just feared, to be influential. But explicit comparisons of the kind scarcely exist. In making a start, we:

1. Survey the scene generally, setting down the scopes in which certain interest-groups appear to be influential according to Procedure A
2. Explore the possibility of reaching some agreement about the relative importance of these scopes. May not (normative) political theory help us here, possibly by furnishing some clues to the public interest, enabling scopes to be ranked?
3. Failing such help, we make an informed judgment of the social significance of each of the relevant scopes; put the pluses and minuses together; and strike a balance.

What, you may say, if the risks known to be involved in Procedure A were unacceptable in particular instances? All the Observer has to go on then in Procedure B is activity, of whose relative social significance he is quite uncertain. Yet he may be pardoned for assuming that intense and probably expensive activity within many scopes, year after year, does indicate relatively considerable influence. Even being wrong about that would probably put him on the right side in terms of the public interest. In the USA some of the state acts regulating lobbying have had little better basis than that—observation of activity as distinct from verification of influence. Here again, however, we could probably increase our understanding of political processes and give a far better account of ourselves as political scientists if we came to the research open-eyed from the modern discussion of influence and power.

DETERMINANTS OF INFLUENCE

Suppose, then, that we could establish (or at least persuade ourselves) that some interest-groups are substantially more influential than others over a certain range: to what would the differences be attributable? It would seem from our code that the differences must arise from differences "in" or "to do with" *PA* and *T*. In a very loose sense, these become the independent variables accounting for the dependent variable, the amount of influence.

GROUP ATTRIBUTES AND NORMS

Differences in Endowments. What is there "about" *PA* that varies in such fashion as to explain variations in the amount of influence? Obviously, interest-groups vary in their endowments. Just what these comprise has never been quite agreed, but except for 2, the following would be almost invariably included:

1. Money and credit
2. (Some properties of) bureaucratic organization
3. Control over jobs
4. Control of supply of expert knowledge
5. Control of supply of votes (through numbers of members)
6. Prestige

No. 2 is often taken for granted but ought not to be. Organizations do vary substantially, even though generically they all belong to the same broad category (= are all secondary groups), and such variations must be expected to make a difference in the amounts of influence exercised. Organizations vary, for example, in cohesiveness, and presumably the more cohesive an organization is, the more it can be wielded as a "hammer" upon the Target. Alternatively put, the more cohesive an organization, the more effective is it likely to be in the face of the Target.

Or take a less elusive dimension than cohesiveness: that which analyzes different communication patterns within organizations in terms of the speed and accuracy of getting work done. Several patterns have been brought into focus, but let the contrast between the *circle* and *star* (or *wheel*), as shown in Figure 7, do duty at first for the reasonably cumulative research of this kind in the last two decades. The circle has commonly been studied on the assumption

Figure 7

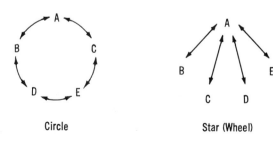

Circle   Star (Wheel)

of "symmetrical linkage," i.e., that Ego (say, A) can communicate with B and C but can reach D and E only indirectly via B and C. Similarly, B can communicate directly only with A and D, and so on. Given such an assumption, it seems reasonably well-established that a star net is more efficient in speed and accuracy of communication than a circle for the simpler, more routine tasks.[22]

Later research changed the emphasis from the communication patterns as such to the interconnected patterns of coordination and decision-making. This meant that the real difference between the circle and star is not, after all, in the communication pattern *as such* but rather in the extent to which the pattern facilitates or obstructs arrangements enabling some one person to coordinate and distribute information. That is to say, *if* a circle got itself quickly organized in that sense of arranging a coordinator, it was not significantly less efficient than a star. The point is that in general a circle obstructs that sort of efficient arrangement. In one experiment, only 3 circles out of 21 developed suitable "hierarchies," whereas all 15 of the stars did so. (As did 17 out of 20 of the *all-channel* nets—those resembling the circle "positionally" but permitting completely free communication—e.g., in the circle diagram above, A can communicate direct with B, C, D, and E.[23]) In a not dissimilar way, the Dutch social scientist Mauk Mulder put his finger less on the nature of the communication-net than on the degree of centralized decision-making. For group performance, a star is usually superior to a circle, but a circle organized to a greater extent than a star in terms of centralized decision-making will "beat" that star.[24] Of course, it still remains true on Mulder's basis that a more centralized star will "beat" a less centralized circle, but according to him it is the degree of centralized decision-making that really counts.

These patterns, as you will have realized or insisted, are no more than highly simplified models, one of which—the "symmetrical linkage" circle—is remote from empirical reality. But professional associations (and Oxford and Cambridge colleges) do have something like all-channel nets, in contrast to the business corporation, which tends to be a "mixed" form, the star principle "lower down" culminating in a pattern not unlike an all-channel net at the very top. The moral is that in our examination of differential influence, we should take into account the internal patterns.

Other structural properties should also be distinguished. Organizations vary in *shape*, meaning the number of levels (of supervision, say) in relation to the total size. If there are relatively few levels, the shape is said to be flat; if many,

[22] The threads may be picked up in Alex Bavelas, "Communication Patterns in Task-oriented Groups," in *Group Dynamics*, 2nd ed., ed. Dorwin Cartwright and Alvin Zander (Row, Peterson & Company, 1960), Chapter 35, and in Harold Guetzkow, Chapter 36 of the same book. Note that for the more complex tasks, the circle tends to be superior to the star, so that in assessing actual endowments we should have to discover the actual nature of the task confronting the organization.

[23] Harold Guetzkow and Herbert A. Simon, *Management Science*, Vol. 1 (1955), as cited by Peter M. Blau and W. Richard Scott, with introduction by J. H. Smith, *Formal Organizations* (London: Routledge & Kegan Paul Ltd., 1966), pp. 126–27.

[24] These writers usually speak of a wheel rather than a star, but I find that students at first confuse a wheel with a circle, for an obvious reason. Mulder's article is in *Sociometry*, Vol. 23 (1960), pp. 1–14.

tall. Classical theory plumped for tall organizations as making for efficient performance; this was related to the belief that the span of control, or management, should be narrow, or close (six, eight, a dozen perhaps, varying mainly with the nature of the tasks to be supervised). Now there is reason to think that flatter organizations may be the more efficient (and, correspondingly, that the span of control should be far wider than was traditionally thought prudent). These are the merest hints of the very substantial work in this field. There is much else, such as the question of morale, which tends, inconveniently, to be higher in the circle than in the star. Morale may be a factor in its own right, or may be somehow related to cohesiveness. Even more crucial perhaps is the capacity of the organization to "learn" to be adaptable. This is the negative "feedback" of cybernetics, but specifically related by leading authorities such as Karl Deutsch to social organizations as well as to communications networks and electronic-control systems. For us the main aspect of "feedback" is the organization's capacity to incorporate "the results of its own action in the new information by which it modifies its subsequent behavior."[25] This may simply entail the adjustments necessary to reach the set goal, but it may also entail modifications of the goal itself. In making adjustments, *lag* may occur; roughly, the time taken to complete corrective action. Now, these ideas (all drawn from Deutsch) are exciting partly because they reintroduce, as he remarked, notions of *purpose*, and so chime in well with a book founded upon interpretations of purposive (or goal-seeking) behavior in Abraham Kaplan's sense;[26] partly because the reintroduction is achieved *without* teleological assumptions of some unchanging goal. But the immediate significance for interest-group studies may be that *lag* has to be interpreted in three ways: (a) the lag characteristic of the organization *as such* in terms of its societal task; (b) the lag in the organization's switch *to* its other self as interest-group; (c) when actually operating as interest-group, the lag in *its* responses to Target-movements and to the movements of other groups as potential allies or rivals. Again, these are only hints; the important thing is to be aware of considerations strangely neglected in the interest-group literature.

The other items on the list of endowments are more or less self-explanatory. The whole list is to be read as provisional; and no one suggests that any particular group (or even any particular type of group) has all these strings to its bow. In the conventional illustration, business groups tend to enjoy in particular items 1-4; trade unions, 5; veterans' associations, 6, derived from some sense of not fully requited "services rendered."[27] Nor should it be assumed that, at any given moment, an endowment can be turned to advantage, since not all endowments are "cashable" in the short run. Other things being equal, that group which enjoys the more versatile set of endowments tends to have the edge on other groups.

---

[25] Karl W. Deutsch, *The Nerves of Government* (New York: The Free Press, 1966), p. 88. See also David Easton, "An Approach to the Analysis of Political Systems," in Ulmer, ed. *Introductory Readings in Political Behavior*, p. 137, and Easton's *A Framework for Political Analysis* (Englewood Cliffs, N. J.: Prentice-Hall, Inc., 1965), pp. 24–25 and 127–30.

[26] See above, pp. 6–8, 27.

[27] See, for Britain, my *The Politics of Influence*: Chapter XXVII, "To Command Success."

Conversion of Endowments. In any case, a group's endowments represent only a potential for use. Clearly, the endowments have to be converted into a form deemed suitable for ventured influence. Granted the available facilities (e.g., the actual development of the mass media if one wishes to undertake PR), then the conversion problem must be mainly normative. In other words, the group's norms determine just how much of its endowments it is willing to allocate to ventured influence. Groups similarly endowed will vary in this respect: it is even conceivable that a group with smaller endowments might allocate absolutely more to ventured influence than some group far better endowed chooses to do. Granted the allocation, groups will vary in the intensity with which it is applied, which might be related to morale, or cohesiveness.

Efficiency in Use. Granted the conversion of endowments, there arises the question of efficiency in use. This is no mere "conversion of energy without loss," but should entail: (a) the identification of the correct Target in the particular instance; and (b) the choice of the best "path" to the Target. Ideally, this ought to constitute a "critical path analysis," charting the necessary sequences and the timing, with the best possible weaving together (in the circumstances) of the instruments, or methods, into which the endowments have been converted. In practice, the procedure is no doubt much more "hit or miss," but no doubt, too, groups vary in the quality of their strategic thinking, planning, and execution.

ORIENTATION OF TARGET

So much for the group itself as (in a loose sense) an independent variable accounting (as a first approximation) for differences in the amount of influence exercised. But, as we have already implied in mentioning Target's normative commitments, Targets are not impassive entities waiting to be manipulated— they are made up of persons, or roles, with distinctive configurations of norms and perceptions (or, at another level of analysis, of political subcultures). Presumably, groups with identical endowments, conversion factors, and efficiencies in use will vary in amounts of influence as Target smiles, or frowns, upon them. This factor is difficult to "separate out" because Target's orientation must relate to group endowments; e.g., Target must, in the long run, be expected to smile upon any group that controls a supply of expert knowledge. Empirically, however, it seems that Target-orientation can be usefully treated as (in a loose sense) an independent variable.

In discussing what lies behind these orientations, we may usefully distinguish between Target as Legislature, and Target as some component of the Executive or Administration. Part of the explanation we require then emerges as follows:

> Where the Target is a Legislature: the legislators' conception of their role as legislators

With an Administration-Target: (a) the administrators' assessment of the social importance of the petitioning group, as judged by societal task; its representativeness; and its "completeness"; and (b) some sense of the "public interest"

Legislature as Target. In England, we have to turn back the clock if we are to think of an autonomous legislature. In the eighteenth century, for instance, interest-groups specifically created "out of doors" were perceived almost as subversive organizations; at best, they were patronized; witness "Prime Minister" Pitt's airy dismissal of the General Chamber of Manufacturers (1785–87) as "a few manufacturers" who had wandered into the "paths of legislation and government,"[28] instead, of course, of keeping to their proper places. Subject to qualification,[29] M.P.'s generally put themselves at the center of the political order, and looked askance (to say the least) at the new associations outside Parliament that were just beginning to feel their feet in this period. They also tended to regard, within the private realm, only the "natural" groups, such as universities and cathedral chapters, as having a legitimate part to play in government. Such norms, if widespread, are inhibiting to the exercise of influence, although not entirely prohibiting.

For a more specific reference we turn to the United States, where John Wahlke and his collaborators questioned 474 legislators in four states (California, New Jersey, Ohio, and Tennessee) during the 1957 legislative session. One of their questions was:

Would you say that, on the whole, the legislature would work [better or worse] if there were no interest groups or lobbies trying to influence legislation?

Why not answer this yourself before proceeding? First decide your general orientation (worse . . . better) and then spell out your answer in terms of: (1) much worse; (2) somewhat worse; (3) about the same; (4) somewhat better; or (5) much better. The answers actually obtained (N = 452) were:

Friendly ←				→ Hostile
1	2	3	4	5
41%	34%	12%	7%	6%

Legislators were also asked:

Do you agree that the job of a legislator is to work out compromises among conflicting interests?

[28] Asa Briggs, *The Age of Improvement* (London: Longmans, Green & Co. Ltd., 1960), p. 117.
[29] Samuel H. Beer, *British Politics in the Collectivist Age* (New York: Alfred A. Knopf, Inc., 1965), Part One.

The answers (N = 462) were (but notice what the numbers now indicate):

1	2	3	4	5
Agree	Tend to agree	Undecided	Tend to disagree	Disagree
31%	42%	2%	12%	13%

On the basis of these answers and of answers to two related questions, and on the basis of answers to a test of legislators' knowledge, or awareness, of lobbying activities, Wahlke and his associates constructed a typology of legislators' *role-orientations* toward interest-groups:

> Facilitators: Friendly and knowledgeable
> Resisters: Hostile and knowledgeable
> Neutrals: (a) Having no strong views, whatever their knowledge; (b) having little knowledge, whatever their views; or (c) having little knowledge and no strong views[30]

The legislators interviewed were then classified in terms of one or other of these three types, whose distribution was worked out for the four state legislatures, as shown in Table 3. Since further analysis disclosed that by no means all Resisters offered a blanket condemnation, the researchers concluded that "pressure politics has become rather widely accepted among legislators in American states."[31] This certainly coincides with my own impressions from interviews with legislators and lobbyists in Massachusetts (1965–66) and Louisiana (1966) as well as with businessmen and PR specialists in California (1961).

[30] The typology is that of Wahlke and his associates; the characterizations of the types are rather crude ones made only for this book. For another typology, see Samuel C. Patterson, "The Role of the Lobbyist: The Case of Oklahoma," *Journal of Politics*, Vol. 25 (February, 1963), pp. 83–92.

[31] John C. Wahlke, William Buchanan, Heinz Eulau, and LeRoy C. Ferguson, "American State Legislators' Role Orientations Toward Pressure Groups," in Ulmer, ed., *Introductory Readings in Political Behavior*, p. 393.

Table 3

Role Orientation	California (N = 97)	New Jersey (N = 78)	Ohio (N = 157)	Tennessee (N = 116)	Total (N = 448)
Facilitators	38%	41%	43%	23%	37%
Neutrals	42	32	35	37	37
Resisters	20	27	22	40	26
	100%	100%	100%	100%	100%

However, for us, the main point is what was done in accordance with the role-orientations. It seems that Facilitators: (a) were more inclined than the others to listen to the groups' representations; (b) tended to give such representations more weight; (c) were more ready to seek lobbyists' help in drafting bills and in other ways.

Now, what we require to know is: Why are Target-orientations to some groups more favorable than to others? If we can answer that, we have another line on differences in the amount of influence exercised. At present, however, we can only speculate that, in a very general way, legislators carry in their heads some sort of ranking system (not unlike that which people have for ranking occupations) that would be found to correspond to the (adjusted) manifestly functional significance of the groups for the inclusive social system. This implies that legislators, perhaps half-consciously, rank groups according to the apparent value of their societal contribution. Thus (in our terminology) interest-groups that are also first-order groups, or anchored in such, will be highly regarded; while groups that are not so located in social space but only peripheral (in functional terms) will, in general, be less highly regarded.

Administration as Target. In trying to elucidate the "meaning" of Target-orientation when the Target is the Administration, we have to confess to an ignorance almost as profound as that revealed in the previous paragraph. The saving "almost" rests (in my case) upon conversations with ministry officials in Britain, and with state administrators in the USA. Let us, however, put this down as no more than a hypothesis, that favorable dispositions on the part of the Administration toward some interest-groups are a function of its perception of: (a) the societal task of the groups; (b) the representativeness of the groups; and (c) the "completeness" of the groups. To (a) I am in no position to add anything. As to (b), some administrators undoubtedly do ask themselves: Is this association representative? The criterion is vague and its lines are shifting, but it is asked, and the more the answer is "yes," the more favorably will the group be regarded. No doubt an association may be representative (in the sense, say, of truly speaking for some sector or field) and yet not amount to much in the eyes of the Administration because the proportions *spoken for* (not to mention the absolute numbers) are inconsiderable. So perception may also be a function of what the German sociologist Simmel called "completeness," a notion which the English political scientist Samuel Finer has (in effect) adapted and given currency to under the name of *density*.[32] The implied question is: What proportion of the potential membership (or "universe") has been recruited (or organized) and so is being *spoken for* "in" this claim? British densities are high (if not as high as the interest-groups would have one believe). A stock contrast is afforded by the density of farm organizations in Britain and the United States: possibly 80 per cent for the National Farmers' Union in England and Wales, as opposed to 30 per

[32] R. M. Blackburn has pointed out that by "completeness" Simmel meant more or less 100 percent, whereas the usual modern concept is that of a proportion. (*Union Character and Social Class* [London: B. T. Batsford Ltd., 1967], p. 14, n. 1.) It is to this concept that in political science the label "density" has been given since at least 1958. Blackburn claims that the use of this term is "incorrect," and takes to task (p. 16, n. 1) Keith Hindell ("Trade Union Membership," *Planning*, Vol. XXVIII, No. 463 [1962] [Political and Economic Planning, London]). According to the argument in Chapter Two above, there can be little question of incorrectness, only (at most) of inconvenience.

cent in the USA—and that "spread over" three or more groups. Another example is that of the former Federation of British Industries, which may have had 85 per cent density in manufacturing (counting firms employing ten or more workers), as opposed to the National Association of Manufacturers' 20-25 per cent (at most) on the same (adjusted) basis.[33] Compare the BDI (Bundesverband der Deutschen Industrie, or Federation of German Industry), claiming 98 per cent of all West German industrialists and composed of 39 industrial associations, not one of which apparently had a density of less than 80 per cent. No doubt the Road Haulage Association in Britain is far more "dense" than the American Trucking Association, which has been said to embody "only a segment of the motor carrier industry."[34]

Even completeness, however, is not in itself decisive: in the minds of the Administration, it is assessed with representativeness in the other, broader sense of *authentic voice*. The British Limbless Ex-Servicemen's Association after World War II was fairly "complete," but for long not regarded as sufficiently representative to be given a seat on the Central Advisory Committee on War Pensions beside the (virtual) nominees of the British Legion. Its representativeness in *that* sense was eventually recognized at a time when it was becoming less complete. Similarly, completeness must also be "read" with societal task. If it is correct to say that the Target (= the Administration), directly or indirectly, does weigh up a petitioning group's societal task, then a peripheral association 100 per cent complete may well enjoy *less* favor than a 40 per cent complete core-association. These factors should be construed as so many throws of the dice. We may suppose the administrator to muse: Is the group making this claim a first-order group or anchored in one? If the answer is "yes": Is it genuinely the spokesman for that sector or realm? If so, how complete is it?

Finally, the Administration's perceptions turn in part upon some sense of the public interest. As the world knows, this is a woolly concept, and certainly it is a controversial one among political scientists. One tradition deriving from Bentley[35] ostensibly denies it any place in the canon: for most writers in this tradition the public interest is a myth, there being simply no comprehensive interest embracing the inclusive sociopolitical system. Without entering into this controversy here, we may note that some administrators do put into the balance some entity that they do call *the public interest*. Often it is expressed in monetary terms: "The country cannot afford it" (as Ministry of Pensions officials kept saying about the British Legion's claim, after the Second World War, to double the basic rate of war pension). But it may well take the form of (*in itself*) reaching a settlement of rival claims. For, of course, Actors often do

[33] Samuel H. Beer, "Group Representation in Britain and the United States," *The Annals,* Vol. 319 (September, 1958), pp. 134–35. The FBI was absorbed in 1965 into the new Confederation of British Industry, which, however, is incomparable with the NAM.

[34] Gerard Braunthal, *The Federation of German Industry in Politics* (Ithaca, N. Y.: Cornell University Press, 1965), p. 31; Robert H. Salisbury, in *Functions and Policies of American Government,* 3rd ed., ed. Jack W. Peltason and James MacGregor Burns (Englewood Cliffs, N. J.: Prentice-Hall, Inc., 1967), p. 135.

[35] Arthur F. Bentley, *The Process of Government* (Chicago: The University of Chicago Press, 1908); Truman, *The Governmental Process;* Charles B. Hagan, "The Group in Political Science," in *Life, Language, Law: Essays in Honor of* Arthur F. Bentley, ed. Richard W. Taylor (Yellow Springs, Ohio: The Antioch Press, 1957), pp. 109–24; Richard W. Taylor, "Arthur F. Bentley's Political Science," *Western Political Quarterly,* Vol. V (June, 1952), pp. 214–30.

have competitors; their claims are advanced, often enough, among a cluster of others, some of which bear directly, others indirectly, upon their own. Administrators may have to choose between them, in part or in whole. And their choice has a cost—the benefit foregone, e.g., a forfeiture of goodwill, a reduction in the supply of specialized information, even a withdrawal of the disappointed group's cooperation. Insofar as the several groups make important social contributions, such decision-costs may be high, and to avoid or minimize these might well be regarded as constituting the public interest.

THE INFLUENCE OF "BUSINESS"

Let us now see if this analysis is at all useful in application. Is there a tiger of "business influence" at large in the jungle, or are the reports of it the imaginings of a credulous people? In the light of the foregoing discussion, we can immediately dismiss "business influence" as such as an empty phrase, and if we tend to dismiss its author too, he has only himself to blame. Not only is "business" (in this connection) much too vague, but at this stage it ought to be a platitude that we discuss a group's influence only in relation to a scope, or range of decisions or policies. What we have to do instead, in terms of the analysis in this book, is to identify "business" at the first-, second-, and third-order levels, which has the effect, since each level embodies something like a characteristic range of claims-decisions, of at least keeping within tolerable bounds the errors tending to arise from the incomparability of scopes.

At the first-order level, what we observe is not business but discrete corporations. Some of these are certainly in direct touch with the Departments; and the larger ones in Britain "may have some independent influence."[36] Evidently, the big American oil companies dominated the National Petroleum Council and may have shown a fairly united front to the Department of the Interior. Generally, it would be surprising if the network of consultation did not confer considerable influence upon those whose advice is so systematically sought. Equally it would be surprising if that advice were always identical, or even similar, and never conflicting. To think otherwise comes from working at too high a level of abstraction; lower your sights and you will see that goals of particular businesses do conflict as well. In the wider sphere, too, particular businesses, like the aircraft companies, can be shown to come off very well with securing contracts, but Hawker Siddeley's gain was BAC's loss; General Dynamics's success was at the expense of Boeing.

At the second-order level, we pick out the industry trade associations, resting ultimately upon the financial support of the relevant companies. For British trade associations, a highly experienced participant and observer, Sir Raymond Street,[37] has asked himself "how far industry, mainly through the trade

---

[36] Leonard Tivey and Ernest Wohlegemuth, "Trade Associations as Interest Groups," *Political Quarterly*, Vol. 29 (January-March, 1958), p. 67.

[37] Chairman of the Cotton Board, 1940–57, and a former Secretary of the Manchester Chamber of Commerce. See "Government Consultation with Industry," *Public Administration* (London), Vol. XXXVII (Spring, 1959), pp. 1–8.

associations, really does influence government policy." His answer may be put down in three parts:

1. Major issues of policy: "not very powerful." Only on "rare occasions" does industry "considerably modify" or reverse "a decision of major policy before legislation is finally passed."
2. The influence of industry (i.e., mainly trade associations) "can become significant again on the detailed application of a major change of policy once that has been irrevocably decided upon."
3. "The influence of industry is extremely effective at all levels below that of major policy decisions."

This answer should not be accepted without some qualification. On part 1 there is room for argument about "major." A former Parliamentary Secretary (Labour) to the Ministry of Transport is evidence for the view that the Roads Campaign Council was "to some extent responsible for the present increased expenditure on our road program. . . ."[38] Was that "major"? Was it even new "policy," or merely the intensification of an existing policy? If it was major policy, then we have to recall that the Roads Campaign Council was largely, though not exclusively, made up of trade associations, including the Society of Motor Manufacturers and Traders, the Motor Agents' Association, the British Road Federation, and the Road Haulage Association itself.[39]

Nor does "modifying" and "reversing" exhaust the forms of influence. There is a fluid and possibly crucial stage before policy has been crystallized. Two of the closest students of trade associations in Britain, Leonard Tivey and Ernest Wohlgemuth, concluded that trade associations "have an indeterminate but profound influence upon the framing of policy by ensuring full awareness of the problems of industry."[40] There is also commitment in advance. In the early post-Second World War period, for example, the Conservatives, then in Opposition, were committed, by the Road Haulage Association, and through the *party* committees in Parliament, to the denationalization of road transport,[41] which the incoming Conservative Government did largely carry out.

To cite such instances is easy; what is more difficult is to decide what proportion of the total flow of major policies they represent. On the whole, taking a long view, Sir Raymond's judgment may not be very far out, always making allowance for the possibility of "profound" influence before policy has been formulated. As for parts 2 and 3, Tivey and Wohlgemuth had already said that trade associations can frequently persuade departments to make changes in specific matters where the policy content is not important, or where it is mainly a case of how the policy is carried out.

Turn now to one "peak," the former Federation of British Industries (FBI),

---

[38] G. R. Strauss, "Pressure Groups I have Known," *Political Quarterly*, Vol. 29 (January-March, 1958), p. 43.

[39] S. E. Finer, "Transport Interests and the Road Lobby," *Political Quarterly*, Vol. 29 (January-March, 1958), pp. 47–48. See also Richard Rose, *Influencing Voters* (London: Faber & Faber Ltd., 1967), p. 144.

[40] "Trade Associations as Interest Groups," p. 68.

[41] Allen Potter, *Organized Groups in British National Politics* (London: Faber & Faber Ltd., 1961), p. 310; Strauss, "Pressure Groups I Have Known."

incorporated since 1965 in the Confederation of British Industry. There can be no doubt that it once enjoyed an extraordinary place in British tariff administration. In 1932 Britain abandoned her free-trade policy. The Act set up an Import Duties Advisory Committee, appointed by the Prime Minister and the Chancellor of the Exchequer (technically, by the Lords Commissioners of the Treasury). This Committee of three distinguished men (in public life in the broad sense, but not officials)[42] was empowered to recommend alterations in duties and in items included in the free list. Recommendations were to go to the Treasury, who could vary these only within narrow limits and who in practice never saw fit to do so throughout the Committee's life (which ended when war came in 1939). Thus the Committee constituted in practice a nonministerial Department, with a civil service staff (by 1938) of about fifty, including nine from the administrative class.[43]

Though free to recommend on its own initiative, the Committee seems in practice to have waited for enlightenment and stimulus by the trade associations. This is where the FBI came in as an adviser to its members in the preparation of applications, for which purpose it established a special department. How far this strategic position vis-à-vis alterations in the tariff structure without reference to Parliament justified the fears of such critics as H. R. G. Greaves[44] is difficult to judge. But we are surely entitled to attach considerable importance to the FBI's role simply in virtue of what it was.

This sketch as so far executed suggests that we should accept a *prima facie* case for the cumulative influence of certain *specified* business *groups* within a certain range. But the issue is not so easily decided. The sketch has defects: it omits failures. Consider, for instance, the National Association of Manufacturers (NAM). Robert Lane and his associates have pointed to the NAM's success in getting the Taft–Hartley Bill passed in 1947, and the extent to which its provisions matched the NAM's claims as expressed in the famous leather-bound booklet with the gold lettering for Congressmen's names, *Now Let's Build America*.[45] But as these commentators well know, that success was preceded by crashing failure in the years up to the United States's entry into the war. In particular, in the New Deal era, of 38 major legislative proposals that became law, the NAM opposed all but seven.[46] Even allowing for some weighting of claims, this cannot be called anything but rout. And it emphasizes again the underlying fact: a business group widely regarded as influential may not be so outside a relatively narrow span of scopes, and, even within these, from time to time suffers very serious defeats.

[42] Lord May (the Sir George May of the 1931 economy cuts); Sir Sidney Chapman, economic historian and economic adviser to the Bank of England; Sir Alan Powell, barrister.

[43] J. W. Grove, *Government and Industry in Britain* (London: Longmans, Green & Co. Ltd., 1962), pp. 332–33.

[44] *Reactionary England and Other Essays* (London: George Allen & Unwin Ltd., 1962). See also Robert A. Brady, *Business as a System of Power* (New York: Columbia University Press, 1943), Chapter V.

[45] Robert E. Lane, James D. Barber, and Fred I. Greenstein, *An Introduction to Political Analysis*, 3rd ed. (Englewood Cliffs, N. J.: Prentice-Hall, Inc., 1962), pp. 94–95.

[46] Alfred S. Cleveland, "NAM: Spokesman for Industry?" *Harvard Business Review*, Vol. 26, No. 3 (May, 1948), pp. 353–71. See also Richard W. Gable, "NAM: Influential Lobby or Kiss of Death?" *Journal of Politics*, Vol. 15 (May, 1953), pp. 254–73, and *The Annals*, Vol. 319 (September, 1958), pp. 88–89.

The implication for the judgment we should reach *on the basis of our sketch* is now clear. Add in the difficulty of not being able to estimate *amount of influence* in the other possible senses ("distance" moved; strength of normative commitment) and all the sketch indicates is that business groups do indeed have substantial influence within certain scopes, *not* that this markedly exceeds the influence of other groups within other scopes. And in the last resort, of course, these scopes are incomparable if we cannot agree upon the underlying values. However, this is not the end of the matter. As political scientists advising statesmen on the regulation of lobbying or some such public question, we should be prepared to act on the informed judgment that business groups, as specified, *are*, in the long run and over a wide span, influential interest-groups in advanced industrial systems of the "mixed" Anglo-American-Australian kind. For that is just what one would expect, on both theoretical and empirical grounds.

Empirically, it would seem to be true that business groups exceed other types numerically;[47] undoubtedly so, if we drop our gaze to take in state politics in the USA.[48] It would also seem that they busy themselves over a greater number of scopes than other types of groups do. At the first-order level, the corporations really have the field to themselves; only they trouble themselves not only with contracts but also with overseas markets, imports, and a score of similar issues. Only they are built so extensively into public administration from that first-order level. This is not true of the other two levels, but, taking the private realm as a whole, it would seem that the specified business groups do "activate" more scopes than any other type of private (secondary) group. It would also seem that business groups are better placed than other types of groups to exert influence in the short run as well as the long, having more versatile endowments. Accordingly, if we were disposed to judge *amount of influence* from observation of the number of Targets aimed at, and from the number of scopes activated in the short as well as the long run, the specified business groups, taken together, would probably be accorded pride of place.

Such a judgment would derive from political art, not political science. It has, however, some foundation not only in scientific analysis, but also in general political-sociological "theory." Think again of the amount of influence as dependent upon the *PA* and *T*. Target is likely to hold in special respect those groups *mainly* responsible for *tackling* the basic societal tasks. But Target itself will be one of that cluster of concrete groups *mainly* responsible for coping with goal-attainment.[49] While all subsystems have exchanges of "facilities" at the boundaries, Target could be pardoned for thinking that the concrete goods and services *it* derives from the economy are especially vital to the achievement of *its* own system-goals. In less peculiar language, government is indebted to the producing groups, immediately and directly, and in a sense not true of other types of private (secondary) groups, for the means of carrying out its own

---

[47] E. E. Schattschneider, *The Semi-Sovereign People* (New York: Holt, Rinehart & Winston, Inc., 1960); Lester Milbrath, *The Washington Lobbyists* (Chicago: Rand McNally & Co., 1963).
[48] Harmon Zeigler, in Herbert Jacob and Kenneth N. Vines, *Politics in the American States* (Boston: Little, Brown and Company, 1965), pp. 109–11.
[49] See above, p. 34.

goals. That government gives much "in return" (an ordered framework at least) is also true, but does not detract from its dependence upon groups undertaking or anchored in what must seem to government the crucial societal task other than its own.

Now this, we hypothesize, gives a head start to interest-groups undertaking or anchored in "production" as opposed to groups deriving from the tasks of pattern-maintenance and integration. But does it serve to discriminate between interest-groups *within* "production"? I think it does because, essential as trade unions are to a civilized economy, they are not the entities, legally or actually, *responsible for* "production." Here we expose the root of (specified) business influence: to governments of whatever ideological bent (in mixed economies), business groups must seem to be the most indispensable of groups in the sense of being *responsible for undertaking* the most indispensable, in the short run, of societal tasks. If (from *PA*) we add to these considerations the probable comparative advantages in endowments, especially in the short run, in conversion factors and efficiencies in use, then we have many reasons for expecting specified business groups to enjoy an overall advantage in the exercise over a wide range of that influence which we think we discern, although by very crude tests, in observation.

THE MULTIPLE
FLOW
OF INFLUENCE

The concept we have used so far was obtained by elucidating nineteenth-century "forms" that were built up (in principle) from observed behaviors and then endowed with convenient names (or signs). Thus the flow of influence was taken to be what I call *simplex*. Just as, in telecommunications, a *simplex* system permits a flow of messages in one direction only (at a time), so the flow of influence we have traced in outline has been from *PA* to *T*, i.e., from Private Actor (other than political party) to (Public) Target. But that scarcely does justice to empirical reality in the twentieth century, at least in some political systems. Unhappily, we have no space left to give the necessary qualifications their due, and must be content here with a very summary justice that is itself a kind of injustice. Among the observed behaviors apparently so relevant that they put the concept under strain are the following:

Duplex Systems. The flow may be what I call *duplex*[1] i.e., *from T to PA*, openly or covertly. Two types of situation may be distinguished. (a) Consider the British food associations set up in the First World War to handle the supply and distribution of meat, fats, and oils: so little were these autonomous that the membership of their governing bodies was subject to the approval of the Ministry of Food, which could control and direct their acts and even dissolve the organizations themselves.[2] The distinguished historian of Unilever,[3] for instance, has recorded that the Soap Makers Federation of 1918, although "in form a voluntary association of manufacturers, was in fact an engine of official

---

[1] In telecommunications, this embodies the notion not only of *opposite direction* but also of simultaneity, which I do not require here. It is just a convenient label for teaching. Do not confuse this with the question of "feedback" as a consequence of public policy, itself the consequence of the interplay between Actor and Target.

[2] Political and Economic Planning, *Industrial Trade Associations* (London: P.E.P. and George Allen & Unwin Ltd., 1957), p. 32.

[3] Charles E. Wilson, cited *ibid.*, p. 13.

compulsion." (*b*) Even where the *PA* of the concept is truly autonomous, a flow may be *duplex*. In the United States, one fairly clearly marked route is from an administrative agency to its own clientele group and from this to congressmen; not Congress as a whole but rather the key committees.[4] In order to maintain or increase their allocation of funds, administrative agencies devise strategies that evidently help them if at the cost of confusing the uninstructed Observer. One agency, for example, made a point of organizing clientele groups in various localities, priming them to engage in approved projects, serving them well, and encouraging them to inform their congressmen of their reaction.[5] Pity the poor researcher who mistook these activities for the initiatives of "git-up-and-go" Americans determined, in the splendid self-help tradition, not to rely upon "The Government" for everything.

These examples involve the Administration; that there may be a *duplex* flow from the legislators was long ago the thesis, if not the language, of the American political scientist James MacGregor Burns. In his six case studies of mainly New Deal and wartime legislation, he found that, with one or two exceptions, no pressure on key congressmen was exerted; on the contrary, they took up positions upon legislation without waiting for pressure from home. In his subsequent book, he remarked upon another kind of initiative, the kind exhibited when a politician stirs up a slumbering interest-group to awareness of the effect of some proposed legislation. "Most" Congressmen

> . . . are in fact lobbyists, but they work at the core of government rather than at the periphery. They are makers of pressures, not merely the subjects of it. They are pressure politicians.[6]

And some of them are better at it, Burns thought, than some recognized lobbyists.

Simplex-Duplex Systems. If, instead of treating the *duplex* in isolation from the *simplex*, we weave them (and so behaviors) together, we have a rather complex pattern that approximates to an empirical instance, the "plays" behind the (U.S.) Employment Act of 1946:

(1) The National Farmers Union in 1944 took an initiative through its president to bring about full-employment legislation.
(2) It was followed up enthusiastically by a Montana senator, one of whose staff assistants, Bertram Gross, was given the task of drafting such a bill.
(3) On an invitation from the congressional side (legislative staff assistant representing a Senate subcommittee), administrative-agency economists joined the "planning team."

[4] Peter Woll, *American Bureaucracy* (New York: W. W. Norton & Company, Inc., 1963), p. 134.

[5] Aaron B. Wildavsky, *The Politics of the Budgetary Process* (Boston: Little, Brown and Company, 1964), reprinted in *Readings in American Political Behavior*, ed. Raymond E. Wolfinger (Englewood Cliffs, N. J.: Prentice-Hall, Inc., 1966), p. 229.

[6] *Congress and the Formation of Economic Policies* (Harvard University thesis, 1947, HU 90:5120. 8A), p. 319; *Congress on Trial* (New York: Harper & Row, Publishers, 1949) pp. 19–20.

So far, the classical concept holds the empirical content well enough, but then, (e.g.):

(4) A congressman whipped up the liberal and labor groups to write to the President (Truman) to ask him to persuade Democratic members of the House Committee on Expenditures in the Executive Departments (the standing committee to which the bill had been referred) to report out, favorably and quickly, on it.

(5) The House Committee on Expenditures, being "bitterly opposed" but having no staff of its own, also sought the aid of outside interest-groups. One congressman, e.g., obtained drafts from the U.S. Chamber of Commerce, the Committee for Economic Development, and from General Motors, not to speak of individuals.[7]

This is a simplified version of events, but it supports Stephen Bailey's conclusion that "a great deal of the soliciting of agency and private interest group aid behind or against the bill throughout its stormy history came from Members of Congress and their staff assistants."[8] For us the great interest lies in what he called "quadruple play," an example of which can be seen at 4, above. This, in isolation, is evidently our *duplex* flow, but going back to the beginning, the picture would rather be:

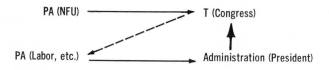

Even that is simplified, for it shows only the gross "pro" movement to the neglect of the "contra" lines emanating from the House Committee; it also fudges the Senate–House distinction, which here is empirically, not conventionally, required. But enough is represented to bring out the marriage of the *simplex* and *duplex* phases. It is one example of Bailey's "shifting coalitions."

Self-contained Systems. Focus now upon the right-hand side of the diagram. In some systems, government works to a "tolerance" (in the engineering sense) that permits, even encourages, a flow of influence that not only originates within the Target-area itself but stays there. This flow I refer to as *self-contained*. In the American case:

---

[7] Stephen Kemp Bailey, *Congress Makes a Law* (New York: Columbia University Press, 1950).

[8] From Bailey's evidence to the Buchanan Committee, Part 1 of *Hearings Before the House Select Committee on Lobbying*, 81st Congress, 2d sess., H. Res. 298, 1950 (Washington: G.P.O., 1950), pp. 31–33. But see also Robert Lane, James D. Barber, and Fred I. Greenstein, *An Introduction to Political Analysis*, 3rd ed. (Englewood Cliffs, N. J.: Prentice-Hall Inc., 1962), Case 17.

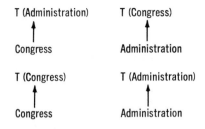

The play between these institutions makes absorbing reading, which cannot, however, be provided here. For us the question is whether both *self-contained* and *duplex* flows should count as manifestations of interest-group activity. An affirmative answer would mean that some components of public secondary groups would have to be reckoned as interest-groups, which would thereupon cease to be the exclusively private entity so far visualized.

This, undoubtedly, is the direction in which a number of political scientists in the United States would wish us to go. Almost at random, we find titles such as "Bureaucracy as a Pressure Group" (Dayton David McKean) or "The Bureaucracy in Pressure Politics" (J. Leiper Freeman).[9] For Gabriel Almond, James Coleman, and their associates, such groups would be species of the genus *institutional interest group*: any "formally organized body made up of professionally employed officials or employees," charged with another function but also performing an interest-articulation function, or constituting "a base of operations for a clique or subgroup" to perform it.[10]

This tradition in the literature carries weight, and it has distinct advantages. For implicitly in general and explicitly in Almond *et al.*, it requires us to ask, as our gaze turns to a political system ostensibly remote from our own: Since it does not seem to have "our" kind of interest-group, and since on general grounds[11] we think the interest-group *work* (or function) has to be undertaken almost everywhere, how it is undertaken in *this* system? By this route we are led to discover that in some systems the articulating and energizing function so far in this book expected mainly of private secondary groups is elsewhere to be traced to some entity within the public realm.

Such an approach is refreshing, especially for those who had the misfortune to be brought up on the old comparative method—country by country, or institution by institution—which was not only wrong, which may be forgivable, but soporific, which hardly ever is. The continuing work in the Almond tradition is all grist to the mill.[12] Even so, I believe that the mill at present

[9] McKean, *Party and Pressure Politics* (Boston: Houghton Mifflin Company, 1949), pp. 597–602; Freeman, *The Annals*, Vol. 319 (September, 1958), pp. 10–19.

[10] *The Politics of the Developing Areas* (Princeton, N. J.: Princeton University Press, 1960), pp. 33–34.

[11] *Ibid.*, Almond's introduction.

[12] E.g., Gabriel A. Almond and Sidney Verba, *The Civic Culture* (Boston: Little, Brown and Company, 1965); Richard Rose, *Politics in England* (Boston: Little, Brown and Company, 1966).

ought to be engaged mainly in producing something resembling what a distinguished sociologist, Robert Merton, called "theories of the middle range." To take the whole wide world as one's domain is to offer too many hostages to fortune. If political science is to remain queen of the sciences, her subjects in Europe and America, and even in Australia, had better cultivate a little humility. In other words, we shall serve the cause best by striving for valid generalizations about Industria; at present we are not exactly groaning under their intolerable weight. If we are burdened, it is with speculations, myths, old wives' tales, and those possibly new wives' tales—the unverified hypotheses about this fundamentally new social system of Industria and the curiously divergent political systems with which it is somehow enmeshed.

Even if that restriction is accepted, however, we have not disposed of the conceptual problem. For the Soviet Union is plainly Advanced Industrian: is the interest-group concept (in its *simplex* form) applicable there, or do we have to concede pride of place to some sort of institutional interest-group? Some groups whose political behavior ostensibly corresponds to the construct have been identified; in descending order of importance, these are: the nuclear scientists, managers of nuclear plants, heads of nuclear services, and those in charge of outer-space experiments; the principal planners and managers of heavy industry and engineering; the trade union leaders, brought together in the All-Union Council of the Trade Unions; the municipalities; the agricultural interest, especially the state-owned (as distinct from the collective) farms; officers of the conventional military forces; some academic leaders; some journalists and writers.[13] If the Brzezinski–Huntington theory of convergence[14] between Soviet and American societies proves to be true, such groups must multiply, each playing a more significant role in the initiation of policy. But that day has not yet dawned.[15] For reasons probably as much historical (especially Muscovite) as ideological, the whole bent of Soviet institutions plainly favors *duplex* and *self-contained* flows. Even for the eight types of groups listed above, the proper paradigm, since they cluster in and around the Central Committee, would be something like:

interest-group ⟶ Central Committee ⟶ Presidium ⟶ Ministries

That is, even if the eight types of group are to be treated as private in the Anglo-American sense of the word, they should probably be located in social space close to the public, or authoritative, institutions. In our paradigm, they

[13] Isaac Deutscher, "Moscow: The Quiet Men: Constellations of Lobbies," *The Nation*, April, 1965, pp. 352–54, 357.

[14] Zbigniew Brzezinski and Samuel P. Huntington, *Political Power: USA/USSR* (New York: The Viking Press Inc., Compass Books, 1965), pp. 9–14.

[15] According to my British clock, it is not even midnight. When Soviet citizens hold a "sit-down" at their equivalent of the Aldermaston Atomic Energy Research Establishment (source of the British Bomb) or of the Microbiological Research Center at Porton (where work on bacteriological warfare is undertaken); or march in large numbers each year from the equivalent of Aldermaston to the heart of Moscow in protest against their own government's defense policy, I shall believe that the hour is at hand.

belong to the righthand side. It has to be recalled, moreover, that the Central Committee itself has, in terms of the concept we have been using, a peculiar status, being a party committee but one so bound to government that we should speak of party-government, which would seem to make our concept of *self-contained* flows of influence peculiarly appropriate. Finally, the range or scope of the decisions that these eight kinds of interest-groups influence appears to be still rather narrow, though on this we are hardly in a good position to judge.

For all these and other reasons, the concept $PA \longrightarrow T : G$ is, at present, of limited usefulness in analyzing the Soviet system, since the implied behavior-patterns are so little represented within it.

Even within some of the liberal-democratic systems, the concept is evidently under strain—from the observation of flows of influence here dubbed *duplex, simplex-duplex,* and *self-contained.* Must, then, we abandon the concept as too frail to carry the mid-twentieth century complexities? If we had to do so, it would not be catastrophic for our exposition in this volume, because the concept as elucidated may (perhaps) be judged to have earned its keep simply as an introductory teaching device. But we ought not to abandon the concept. In the first place, we simply do not know the extent to which, not only in the United States but in other liberal-democracies, the actual influence-flows diverge from the "original," *simplex* model. In other words, what are the *simplex : duplex/ simplex-duplex/self-contained* proportions? We have some evidence already bearing on this issue. For instance, in terms of the *simplex : simplex-duplex* ratio, we have the judgment of Stephen Bailey that "quadruple play" is unusual but that "double and triple plays initiated by, *or with assists by,* Members of Congress are not all that unusual."[16] For us, however, the words italicized (by me) leave the issue open, since the identification of the initiating sources is crucial. To the extent that the initiating and energizing source is still *PA,* then, however complicated the subsequent choreography, the concept would be worth saving. Again, a substantial literature in public administration and related categories bears upon the extent of the *self-contained* flows, notably in the United States. In general, however, and even for the United States, we need much more research into that astonishingly neglected subject, the springs of public policy in liberal-democratic systems, before we need think seriously about jettisoning what we already have on hand. Meanwhile, we have only to ask: Are the actions (or behaviors) "contained" in the *simplex* concept still observable in the Anglo-American-French type of system? If so, are they important? The answer in both cases is obviously "yes." Although we cannot yet say how important, such actions (and so such groups) are certainly crucial to our understanding of the formulation and execution of public policy. If so, we still need a "cut-off" from that flow of interactions which is empirical reality, and this is just what the interest-group concept (in its *simplex* form) provides.

Second, even if research did disclose that the *duplex, simplex-duplex,* and *self-contained* flows were *generally* significant, I should be inclined to oppose their assimilation to the interest-group concept except, perhaps, at a very high level of abstraction. We began our discussion by trying to distinguish different

16 *Congress Makes a Law,* p. 31.

"things"[17] and then naming them, fancy free in principle if not in practice. The *simplex* activity *is* a different "thing" from the other activities: as the German political scientist Wolfgang Hofman, discussing interest-groups, has well said, this "thing" entails "private demands on public means."[18] The nature of the Actor in *interest-group* being so different from that of Actor in the public domain, the styles of action must be so different as to be incomparable. At the same time the attempt to measure influence would also fail for incomparability: of Actor, level, *scope*, and Target. So even if the classical concept were extended, the gain would probably be illusory because the classical discriminations would still have to be made; that is, the two realms—public and private—would still have to be distinguished and dealt with separately before we could have a valid discussion. The *duplex* and other notions are useful for sensitizing us to the complexities of policy-making in some political systems, so that we automatically look beyond the *simplex* to the wider sources of it. In other words, we are reminded that *interest-groups* (as understood here) constitute only one of the sources of public policy. But by the same token we are also reminded that interest-group activity *is* a different "thing." Different "things" require different names, which is where we came in.

[17] See above, pp. 3–6, 13.
[18] "The Public Interest Pressure Group: The Case of the Deutsche Städtetag [German Association of Cities and Towns]," *Public Administration* (London), Vol. 45 (Autumn, 1967), p. 245.

To explore further

This is neither comprehensive nor even a list of "the hundred best books" but simply a means of keeping up the momentum in the direction we have been going in this volume, although in due course I do point out alternative routes. If possible, first strengthen your grasp of fundamentals. *Abstraction*: S. I. Hayakawa, *Language in Thought and Action*, 2nd ed. (New York: Harcourt, 1963, and London: Allen and Unwin, 1965), Chaps. 10–12. But be sure to correct for the "meaning" of (abstracted) behavior: consult the authors in notes 1 and 2, Chap. Two, including Heinz Eulau in *The Limits. . . . Analysis* (as treated in this volume): Pursue the notion of the courts as Public Targets, via notes 17–19, Chap. Three, taking in Fred V. Cahill, *Judicial Legislation* (New York: Ronald, 1952), and Lucius J. Barker, "The Supreme Court as Policy-Maker: The Tidelands Oil Controversy," *Journal of Politics*, Vol. 24 (May, 1962). *Synthesis* (as here treated): Side-step for the time being Maine, Tönnies, and Parsons, and get your bearings from F. X. Sutton and Seymour Martin Lipset (notes 26 and 25, Chap. Three). *Culture*: Clyde Kluckhohn, "Culture and Behavior," in *Handbook of Social Psychology*, Vol. II, ed. Gardner Lindzey (Reading, Mass.: Addison-Wesley, 1954), and "The Study of Culture" (as in note 3, Chap. Four). *Political Culture*: See Almond, and Beer, *et al.* (note 4, Chap. Four); then consider the views of Young C. Kim, "The Concept of Political Culture in Comparative Politics," *Journal of Politics*, Vol. 26 (1964), pp. 313–36. See also Francis G. Castles, *Pressure Groups and Political Culture* (London: Routledge, and New York: Humanities, 1967).

If you cannot at present find time for such background reading, then pick up the trail of specific interest-groups in various political systems. You need this more detailed knowledge partly in order to test my schema of the determinants of styles of action but also for general use independently of that schema. Focus first upon the two systems touched upon in the text. The detailed literature for the United States tends to engulf one, but take as "anchor man" Harmon

Zeigler, in (1) *Interest Groups in American Society* (Englewood Cliffs, N. J.: Prentice-Hall, 1965), starting for this purpose with Chap. IV, and (2) "Interest Groups and the States," in *Politics and the American States*, ed. Herbert Jacob and Kenneth N. Vines (Boston: Little, Brown, 1965). Next, go to David Truman's selected bibliography (Sections 2, 3, and 4) in the landmark book of the postwar years, *The Governmental Process* (New York: Knopf, 1951), for references up to about 1950. Then add to it from the bibliography in Zeigler (2), and as follows: *The Annals*, Vol. 319 (September, 1958), ed. Donald C. Blaisdell, and Vol. 179 (May, 1935), ed. Harwood L. Childs. For readers of French: Léon Dion, *Les Groupes et le pouvoir politique aux Etats-Unis* (Québec: Les Presses de l'Université Laval, and Paris: Armand Colin, 1965); Douglass Cater, *Power in Washington* (London: Collins, 1965); Lester W. Milbrath, *The Washington Lobbyists* (Chicago: Rand McNally, 1963); Paul W. Cherington and Ralph L. Gillen, *The Business Representative in Washington* (Washington: Brookings Institution, 1962); Karl Schriftgiesser, *The Lobbyists* (Boston: Little, Brown, 1951); Walton Hamilton, *The Politics of Industry* (New York: Knopf, 1957); Robert Engler, *The Politics of Oil* (New York: Macmillan, 1961); Joseph C. Palamountain, Jr., *The Politics of Distribution* (Cambridge, Mass.: Harvard, 1955); Harmon Zeigler, *The Politics of Small Business* (Washington, D. C.: Public Affairs Press, 1961); John H. Bunzel, *The American Small Businessman* (New York: Knopf, 1962); Richard W. Gable, "NAM: Influential Lobby or Kiss of Death?" *Journal of Politics*, Vol. 15 (May, 1953), and "Political Interest Groups as Policy Shapers," *The Annals*, Vol. 319 (September, 1958); Marver Bernstein, "Political Ideas of Selected American Business Journals," *Public Opinion Quarterly*, Vol. XVII (Summer, 1953); Oliver Garceau and Corinne Silverman, "A Pressure Group and the Pressured: A Case Report," *American Political Science Review*, Vol. XLVIII (September, 1954); Earl Latham, *The Group Basis of Politics* (Ithaca: N. Y.: Cornell, 1952); Marshall E. Dimock, *Business and Government* (New York: Holt, 1953); Raymond A. Bauer, Ithiel de Sola Pool, and Lewis Anthony Dexter, *American Business and Public Policy* (New York: Atherton, 1963); Robert E. Lane, *The Regulation of Businessmen* (New Haven: Yale, 1953); *The Politics of Regulation*, ed. Samuel Krislov and Lloyd D. Musolf (Boston: Houghton Mifflin, 1964); Andrew Hacker, *Politics and the Corporation* (New York: Fund for the Republic, 1958); Grant McConnell, *Private Power and American Democracy* (New York: Knopf, 1966), Chap. 8; Robert A. Dahl, "Business and Politics: A Critical Appraisal of Political Science," *American Political Science Review*, Vol. LIII (March, 1959).

Compared with business, American trade unions *as interest-groups* seem to have received less treatment in depth. Add to David Truman's list: Avery Leiserson, "Organized Labor as a Pressure Group," in *Labor in the American Economy*, ed. Gordon S. Watkins, *The Annals*, Vol. 274 (March, 1951); James B. Carey, "Organized Labor in Politics," in *The Annals*, Vol. 319 (September, 1958); Fay Calkins, *The C.I.O. and the Democratic Party* (Chicago: University of Chicago, 1952); Arthur Kornhauser, Harold L. Sheppard, and Albert J. Mayer, *When Labor Votes* (New Hyde Park, N.Y.: University Books, 1956); Seymour M. Lipset, *Political Man* (London: Heinemann, 1960), Chap. IX; J. David Greenstone, "Party Pressure on Organized Labor in Three Cities," in *The Electoral Process*, ed. M. Kent Jennings and L. Harmon Zeigler (Englewood Cliffs, N. J.: Prentice-Hall,

1966); Harold Wilensky, "The Labor Vote," *Social Forces*, Vol. XXXV (December, 1956); Gerald Pomper, "The Public Relations of Organized Labor," *Public Opinion Quarterly*, Vol. XXIII (Winter, 1960). *Farm*: Charles M. Hardin, *The Politics of Agriculture* (Glencoe Ill.: Free Press, 1952); Wesley C. McCune, *Who's Behind Our Farm Policy?* (New York: Praeger, 1956); Christiana M. Campbell, *The Farm Bureau and the New Deal* (Urbana, Ill.: University of Illinois, 1962); Don F. Hadwiger and Ross B. Talbot, *Pressures and Protests: The Kennedy Farm Program and the Wheat Referendum of 1963* (San Francisco: Chandler, 1965); J. Roland Pennock, "Agricultural Subsidies in England and the United States," *American Political Science Review*, Vol. LVI (September, 1962). On the wider issue, see Grant McConnell, *The Decline of Agrarian Democracy* (Berkeley: University of California, 1953), and A. Whitney Griswold, *Farming and Democracy*, 2nd ed. (New Haven: Yale, 1963).

Miscellaneous: Mary R. Dearing, *Veterans in Politics: The Story of the GAR* (Baton Rouge: Louisiana State University, 1952); Roscoe Baker, *The American Legion and Foreign Policy* (New York: Bookman Associates, 1954); Albert Somit and Joseph Tanenhaus, "The Veteran in the Electoral Process: The House of Representatives," *Journal of Politics*, Vol. 19 (May, 1957). Luke E. Ebersole, *Church Lobbying in the Nation's Capital* (New York: Macmillan, 1951). Abraham Holtzman, *The Townsend Movement: A Study in Old Age Politics* (New York: Bookman Associates, 1963); Frank A. Pinner, Paul Jacobs, and Philip Selznick, *Old Age and Political Behavior* (Berkeley: University of California, 1959); LeRoy Bowman, *The American Funeral* (Washington, D. C.: Public Affairs Press, 1959). Stanley Kelley, Jr., *Professional Public Relations and Political Power* (Baltimore: Johns Hopkins, 1956), supplemented (and on a few points of detail corrected by later information) by *The Role of Public Relations in Political Campaigns*, transcript of testimony by Clem Whitaker and Leone Baxter before the United States Senate Special Committee on Political Activities, Lobbying and Campaign Contributions, San Francisco, January, 1957. R. Joseph Monsen, Jr., and Mark W. Cannon, *The Makers of Public Policy: American Power Groups and Their Ideologies* (New York: McGraw-Hill, 1965). Robert A. Dahl, *Congress and Foreign Policy* (New York: Harcourt, 1950); Charles S. Campbell, *Special Business Interests and the Open Door Policy* (New Haven: Yale, 1951); Bernard C. Cohen, *The Political Process and Foreign Policy: The Making of the Japanese Peace Settlement* (Princeton, N. J.: Princeton University, 1957), and *The Influence of Non-Governmental Groups on Foreign Policy-Making* (Boston: World Peace Foundation, 1959); Gabriel A. Almond, "Public Opinion and National Security Policy," *Public Opinion Quarterly*, Vol. XX (Summer, 1956); Franklin L. Burdette, "The Influence of Noncongressional Pressures on Foreign Policy," *The Annals*, Vol. 289 (September, 1953); Donald C. Blaisdell, "Pressure Groups, Foreign Policies, and International Politics," *The Annals*, Vol. 319 (September, 1958).

For Britain, see J. D. Stewart, *British Pressure Groups* (Oxford: Clarendon, 1958), noting his "Notes on Sources," and S. E. Finer, *Anonymous Empire*, 2nd ed. (London: Pall Mall Press, 1966), consulting his bibliography. Then add or amend as follows: John H. Millett, "British Interest-Group Tactics: A Case Study," *Political Science Quarterly*, Vol. LXXII (March, 1957), and "The Role of an Interest Group Leader in the House of Commons," *Western Political Quarterly*, Vol. IX

(December, 1956); Peter Self and Herbert J. Storing, *The State and the Farmer* (London: Allen and Unwin, 1962); Peter G. Richards, *Honorable Members*, 2nd ed. (London: Faber, 1964), Chaps. 7–10. J. W. Grove, *Government and Industry in Britain* (London: Longmans, 1962), Introduction and especially Part One; J. J. Richardson, "The Making of the Restrictive Trade Practices Act, 1956—A Case Study of the Policy Process in Britain," *Parliamentary Affairs*, Vol. XX (Autumn, 1967); A. R. Ilersic, assisted by P. F. B. Little, *Parliament of Commerce* (London: Association of British Chambers of Commerce and Newman Neame Ltd., 1960). Richard Rose's *Influencing Voters* (London: Faber, 1967) is a basic work, as is Allen Potter's *Organized Groups in British National Politics* (London: Faber, 1961). For a discussion of how far the works published up to the early Sixties adequately covered the ground, see Morris Davis, "Some Neglected Aspects of British Pressure Groups," *Midwest Journal of Political Science*, Vol. VII (February, 1963). Then set the whole activity in perspective through Samuel H. Beer's outstanding study, *British Politics in the Collectivist Age* (New York: Knopf, 1965), which appeared in Britain as *Modern British Politics* (Faber, 1965).

Many paths now beckon. *Australia*: W. A. Townsley in *Interest Groups on Four Continents*, ed. Henry W. Ehrmann (Pittsburgh: University of Pittsburgh Press, 1958); A. F. Davies in *The Government of Australian States*, ed. S. R. Davis (London: Longmans, 1960); Josephine F. Milburn and Taylor Cole, "Bibliographical Material on Political Parties and Pressure Groups in Australia, New Zealand, and South Africa," *American Political Science Review*, Vol. LI (March, 1957).

Canada: Chapter 5 in Frederick C. Engelmann and Mildred A. Schwartz, *Political Parties and the Canadian Social Structure* (Scarborough, Ontario: Prentice-Hall, of Canada, 1967). For the older British Commonwealth generally: Josephine F. Milburn, *Governments of the Commonwealth* (New York: Harper, 1965).

Federal Republic of Germany: Wolfgang Hirsch-Weber in *Interest Groups on Four Continents*, ed. Henry W. Ehrmann; Gerard Braunthal, *The Federation of German Industry in Politics* (Ithaca, N. Y.: Cornell, 1965); Gabriel A. Almond, "The Political Attitudes of German Business," *World Politics*, Vol. VIII (January, 1956); Ronald F. Bunn, "The Federation of German Employers' Associations: A Political Interest Group," *Western Political Quarterly*, Vol. XIII (September, 1960). Also consult: Karl W. Deutsch and Lewis J. Edinger, *Germany Rejoins the Powers: Mass Opinion, Interest Groups, and Elites in Contemporary German Foreign Policy* (Stanford: Stanford University, 1959); U. W. Kitzinger, *German Electoral Politics: A Study of the 1957 Campaign* (Oxford: Clarendon, 1960).

France: If you read French easily, dip into Jean Meynaud, *Les Groupes de pression en France* (Paris: Armand Colin, 1958) and then peruse *Nouvelles Etudes sur les groupes de pression en France* (Paris: Armand Colin, 1962). Otherwise, pick up from Chapter 20 of Philip Williams, *Politics in Post-War France* (London: Longmans, 1954) and Chapters 25 and 26 of his *Crisis and Compromise* (Longmans, 1964), different editions of the same book but worth following through as published. *Business*: The leading work is still Henry W. Ehrmann, *Organized Business in France* (Princeton: Princeton University, 1957), of which a French version (Paris: Armand Colin) appeared in 1959. A useful supplementation is "Le Syndicalisme Patronal," Chap. II of Jean-Daniel Reynaud, *Les Syndicats en France* (Paris: Armand Colin, 1963). *Trade unions*: Val R. Lorwin, *The French Labor Movement* (Cambridge, Mass.: Harvard, 1954), and Jean-Daniel Reynaud, *op. cit.* When (and, I suggest, *only* when) you have read most of the above-mentioned works in English, you should turn to George E. Lavau, "Political Pressures by Interest Groups in France" in *Interest Groups on Four Continents*, ed. Henry W. Ehrmann. As a corrective to overemphasis of the role of interest-groups in the Fifth Republic, consult F. R. Ridley, "French Technocracy and Comparative Government," *Political Studies*, Vol. XIV (February, 1966), especially pp. 39 and 44.

Italy: The basic work is Joseph LaPalombara, *Interest Groups in Italian Politics* (Princeton, N. J.: Princeton University, 1964). *Trade unions*: Joseph A. LaPalombara, *The Italian Labor Movement: Problems and Prospects* (Ithaca, N. Y.: Cornell University, 1957); Daniel L. Horowitz, *The Italian Labor Movement* (Cambridge, Mass.: Harvard, 1963).

The Netherlands: Alan Robinson, *Dutch Organized Agriculture in International Politics, 1945–60* (The Hague: Martinus Nijhoff, 1961).

Norway: Knut Dahl Jacobsen, "Public Administration under Pressure: The Role of the Expert in the Modernization of Traditional Agriculture," *Scandinavian Political Studies*, Vol. 1, 1966 (Helsinki: Academic Bookstore; New York and London: Columbia University Press, 1966).

Sweden: Gunnar Heckscher, "Group Organization in Sweden," *Public Opinion Quarterly*, Vol. III (January, 1939), and in *Interest Groups on Four Continents*, ed. Henry W. Ehrmann.

USSR: For the purpose in hand, you might start with Zbigniew Brzezinski and Samuel P. Huntington (see note 14 in Chap. Six), especially Chapter four, and go on to Isaac Deutscher (see note 13).

Yugoslavia: Country report by Jovan Djirdjevic in *Interest Groups on Four Continents*, ed. Henry W. Ehrmann; Najdan Pasíc, "Groups of Interest and Yugoslav Political Practice" (paper presented to VIth Congress of the International Political Science Association, 1964).

With all this information under your belt, you will be better able to judge the adequacy of my analysis of the determinants of styles of action, and to consider other formulations, in particular: Harry Eckstein, *Pressure Group Politics* (London: Allen and Unwin, 1960), Chap. I; compare his analysis with Richard J. Willey's, "Pressure Group Politics: The Case of Sohyo," *Western Political Quarterly*, Vol. XVII (December, 1964); Gabriel A. Almond, "The Comparative Study of Interest Groups and the Political Process," *American Political Science Review*, Vol. LII (March, 1958); Francis G. Castles, *op. cit.*

On the influence of interest-groups (which could be "operationalized" independently of any particular schema of determinants), see Robert A. Dahl, Chap. Three of *Modern Political Analysis*, 2nd ed., in this series. Then contrast Martha Derthick, *The National Guard in Politics* (Cambridge, Mass.: Harvard, 1965), pp. 6–14. If you are convinced by Professor Dahl (and me, pp. 74–75), you might now, as an exercise, select an instance of "issue-convergence" (see pp. 80–82), and work it out as a case study of differential influence. This is the stage at which you have to try out your own wings, thinking for yourself and starting to formulate tentative hypotheses about the relationship between things. For inspiration, turn to Samuel J. Eldersveld's outstanding paper in *Interest Groups on Four Continents*, ed. Henry W. Ehrmann. But in the last resort you are on your own. Cultivate the habit not of accumulating "facts" in the encyclopedic sense but of looking for relationships not only between what are already recognized as facts but also between an existing fact and one not yet or only dimly perceived, brought to the surface by your expectation (or hypothesis). In other words, read "horizontally," within the limits of conventional "subjects," across subjects, and across political systems.

INDEX

B after entry = Britain

Abrams, Mark, 59
Abstraction:
  as kind of real definition, 4, 5
  ladder, 9, 10, 11, 23, 24
  as real definition of interest group,
    8–13, 18, 30
  stage-one (= semantic
    interpretation), 8
Académie Française, 35
Act, as raw behavior, 8
Action:
  derived from interpretation of acts,
    8
  as "units" (= data) of political
    science, 8
Action, styles of (*see* Styles of action)
Actor, Private (*see* Interest-group)
Adaptation, as pattern variable, 33,
  95
Advertising, political, 50, 51, 51n
  (*see also* Public Relations)
AFL–CIO, 81
Aims of Industry Limited (B), 40, 70,
  71, 71n
Almond, Gabriel A., 59, 99
American Academy of Arts and
  Sciences, 35
American Anti-Slavery Society, 11
American Bar Association, 37
American Legion, 42
American Petroleum Institute, 40, 72

American Philosophical Society, 35
American Trucking Association, 90
Amery, L. S., 58
Analysis:
  as kind of real definition, 4–5
  as real definition of interest group,
    20–27, 30
"Anchorage," 38, 39, 40, 43, 44, 89,
  95
Anderson, Totton J., 2
Anti-Corn Law League (B), 39
Anti-Saloon League, 17, 21, 22n, 40
Anti-Slavery Society (B), 11
Anti-Slavery Society for the
    Protection of Human Rights
    (B), 43
Appropriations Committee, 55
Apter, David A., 22
Armed Services Committees, 54, 55
Army Corps of Engineers, 67
Associated Chambers of
    Manufacturers (Australia), 37
Association of Agriculture (B), 40
Association of American Railroads,
  72
Association of Assistant Mistresses in
    Secondary Schools (B), 38
Association of British Chambers of
    Commerce, 37
Association of Women Doctors
    (France), 38

Attitude group, 1, 43, 43n, 44
Attitudes, and group norms, 43n

Bagehot, Walter, 57
Bailey, Stephen Kemp, 98, 101
Beer, Samuel H., 57
Behavior, social meaning of, 6–8
Behavioralism, late 1960's, 7n, 80n
Bentley, Arthur F., 90
Black, Max, 3
Blackburn, R. M., 89n
Black Power, influence in Britain,
    41, 44
Boeing Aircraft Company, 51, 52, 53,
    66, 78, 91
British Academy of Forensic Science,
    35
British Aircraft Corporation, 51–52,
    91
British Council of Churches, 37
British European Airways, 51, 52
British Legion, 39, 42, 90
British Limbless Ex-Servicemen's
    Association, 90
British Nuclear Energy Society, 35
British "political fringe," 43
British Psychological Society, 35
British Road Federation, 92
British tariff administration, and
    Federation of British Industries,
    92–93
British Trawlers' Federation (Distant
    Water Section), 71–72
British Union for the Abolition of
    Vivisection, Inc., 43
Brogan, Sir Denis, 53
Bryce, James, 2
Bund der Heimatvertriebenen und
    Entrechteten, 21
Bundesverband der Deutschen
    Industrie, 37, 40, 90
Bureaucracy as interest-group, 99
Bureaucratic organization:
    as interest-group endowment, 83
    properties of, 83–85
Burke, Edmund, 55
Burns, James MacGregor, 97
"Business," influence of, 91–95
Business Advisory Council (see
    Business Council)
Business and Defense Services
    Administration, 63
Business Council, 62, 65

Cabinet:
    American and British, 66
    British:
        aircraft contract decision, 51
        stability, 57–58
Campaign Against Racial
    Discrimination (B), 44
Campaign for Democratic Socialism
    (B), 44
Campaign for Nuclear Disarmament
    (B), 43–44
Campbell, Angus, 53, 54
Canadian Chamber of Commerce,
    37
Canadian Manufacturers' Association,
    37
Caribbean Association (B), 41
Cartwright, Dorwin, 74
Catalytic group, 1, 2
Catholic Church (France), 40
Cause group, 39 (see also Idea-
    group)
Celler Committee, 62
Center Party (Sweden), and farmers,
    22
Central Advisory Committee on War
    Pensions (B), 90
Childs, Harwood L., 39
Citizens' Industrial Association of
    America, 39
Civil Aeronautics Board, 64
Civil Service Clerical Association (B),
    26
Classification:
    as distinct from division, 15n
    of interest-groups, 30–44
Clayton Act, 81
Clientelism:
    in Britain, 65–67
    in USA:
        administrative agencies, 97
        Commissions, 64–65
        Departments, 63–64
Coleman, James, 99
Comité de Prévoyance et d'Action
    Sociale, 40
Committee for Economic
    Development, 72, 98
"Completeness," 87, 89, 90
Comrades of the Great War (B), 39
Confederation of British Industry, 24,
    37, 93
    Industrial Policy Group, 24

Confédération Française des
    Travailleurs Chrétiens, 81
Confédération Générale du Patronat
    Français (see Conseil National
    du Patronat Français)
Confédération Générale de la
    Production Française (see
    Conseil National du Patronat
    Français)
Confédération Générale du Travail,
    81
Confederazione Generale
    dell'Industria Italiana
    (Confindustria), 37
Confederazione Generale Italiana del
    Lavoro, 22
Confederazione Italiana Sindacati
    Lavoratori, 22
Confindustria (Italy), 37
Conseil National du Patronat
    Français, 37, 39–40, 81
Conservative Party (B), and Road
    Haulage Association, 70, 92
Conservative Party (Sweden), and
    white-collar workers, 22
Cooley, C. H., 31
Co-option in Government, virtual:
    official:
        advisory committees, USA, 62–63
        in Britain, 65
    de facto (= clientelism), 63–67
        (see also Clientelism)
Courts of law, as Public Targets,
    25–26
Culture:
    covert, 59
    defined, 45
    political:
        defined, 46
        "defining the situation," 47
        an immediate determinant of
            style of action, 46, 55, 56–62
Cybernetics:
    negative "feedback," 85
    "lag," in interest-group analysis, 85

Dahl, Robert A., 25, 74, 76, 78, 79
Davis, Kingsley, 32
Defense Department, 66, 78
Definition, kinds of, 2–5
    nominal, 3–4, 30
        lexical, reported, descriptive, 3–4
        stipulative, stipulated, 3–4

Definition, kinds of (cont.)
    real, 3–5, 30, 73
        abstraction, 4–5
        analysis, 4–5
        essence, 4
        synthesis, 4–5
"Definition of the situation," 47
de Grazia, Alfred, 18
Democrazia Cristiana, 22
Dempsey, Jack, 78
"Density," 89, 89n, 90
Department of Agriculture, 63, 66
Department of Commerce, 62, 63, 66
Department of Labor, 63, 66
Derthick, Martha, 74–75
Deutsch, Karl W., 85
Deutsche Städtetag, 102n
Duke of Windsor (see Wales, Prince
    of)
"Duplex" flow (see Influence, flows
    of)
Duverger, Maurice, 60, 61, 62

Eckstein, Harry, 3n, 17, 18, 44, 57, 58,
    61
Economic League (B), 40, 70, 71
Emmet, Dorothy, 23
Employment Act of 1946, 97–98
Equal Rights (B), 44
Essences, 4, 15, 24, 26, 44
Executive government, suspicion of,
    "interwoven" in British
    Constitution, 58

Fabian Society (B), 20–21
Farmers, Swedish, and Center party,
    22
Federal Reserve System, 67
Federation of Agriculture
    (Netherlands), 37
Federation of British Industries, 90
    in British tariff administration,
        92–93 (see also Confederation
        of British Industry)
Federation of German Industry, 37,
    40, 90
Federation of Labor (Sweden), and
    Social-Democratic party, 22
"Feedback":
    negative, 85
    and policy, 47, 96n
Finer, Samuel E., 2, 16, 17n, 89
Firth, Raymond, 6, 7

Flows of influence (see Influence, flows of)
F-111 (see TFX)
Freeman, J. Leiper, 99
Functionalism, 31–36, 99

Gemeinschaft, 28, 29, 31n, 45
General Chamber of Manufacturers (England), 87
General Dynamics Corporation, 51, 52, 53, 66, 78, 91
Genetic Study Unit (B), 39, 43
George V, King, rebukes Prince of Wales, 42
Gesellschaft, 28, 29, 31n, 45
Goal-Attainment, as pattern variable, 33, 94
Greaves, H. R. G., 93
Gross, Bertram M., 2, 97
Group, social (see also Pressure group):
    norms, 43n
    primary, 30–31, 31n, 35
    secondary, 16, 30–31, 31n, 35, 45, 83
        operational units, 37, 38, 38n
        structure "above" operational units, 37–38
Group Representation Before Congress, 17
Grumman Aircraft Engineering Corporation, 53

Hawker Sieldeley Aviation (B), 51, 52, 91
Heckscher, Gunnar, 22
Hempel, Carl, 3
Himmler, 42
Hindell, Keith, 89n
Hitler, 42
Hobson, E. W., 7
Hofman, Wolfgang, 102
House Committee on Expenditures in the Executive Departments, 98
Howard League for Penal Reform (B), 43
Hunt, N. C., 2
Huntington, Samuel P., 100
Hurry, Colin, opinion survey in Britain, 69

Idea-group, 39, 43
Import Duties Advisory Committee (B), 93

Independent Commissions, 64, 67
Independent Labour party (B), 20–21
Indian Workers' Association (B), 39, 41
Industrial Policy Group (B), 24
Influence:
    of "Business," 91–95
    concept, 96
    flows of:
        duplex, 96–97, 101, 102
        "quadruple play," 98, 101
        self-contained, 98–99, 101
        simplex, 96, 100 (concept under strain, 100–101)
        simplex–duplex, 97–98, 101
    of interest-groups (see Influence of interest-groups)
Influence of interest-groups:
    comparability, 73, 78, 80–82, 91, 101, 102
    determinants of, 82–91
        group attributes and norms, 83–86 (endowments, 83–85; conversion of endowments, 86; efficient use of endowments, 86)
        orientation of Target to group, 86–90
    measures, 76–79, 102
        operationalized, 79–82
Inkeles, Alex, 32
Inns of Court (B), 37
Institute of Industry (German Federal Republic), 40
Institute of Public Relations (B), 67
Integration, as pattern variable, 33, 95
Interest, an, 18
Interest-group:
    attributes, 83–86
    bureaucracy as, 99
    classification, 30–44
        in Childs, Eckstein, Meynaud, 39, 44
        core-groups, 40
        institutional, 99, 100
        other-regarding, 27
        peripheral, 41–44 (achieved, 43–44; ascribed, 41–43)
        selfish, 27
        self-regarding, 27
        unselfish, 27
    comparability, 73, 78, 80–82, 91, 101, 102

Interest-group (*cont.*)
  component of type of society,
    27–30
  concept:
    limits of, 41, 43–44, 100–101
    private *v.* public, 35, 102
  functional significance, 35–36, 38,
    40, 44, 89, 90
  orientation to, by Target, 86–91
  and parties, 22–23, 92
  and political culture, 46, 55–62
  representativeness, in Target's eyes,
    89–90
  role:
    principal, 23
    representative (broker, 23–24;
      spokesman, 23–24)
  term, 13–19 (early use, 17)
Interest group, political, 1, 17
Interstate Commerce Commission, 64
Issue-convergence, cases for research,
  80–82

Jones, Jesse, 63

Kaplan, Abraham, 8, 27, 76, 85
Krislov, Samuel, 18

Labor–Management Relations (Taft–
  Hartley) Act of 1947, 69, 81,
  93
Labor–Management Reporting and
  Disclosure (Landrum-Griffin)
  Act of 1959, 81
Labour party (B):
  and Campaign for Nuclear
    Disarmament, 44
  and trade unions, 20–21
Labour Representation Committee
  (B), 20–21
"Lag," as factor in differential
  influence, 85
Lane, Edgar, 2, 16
LaPalombara, Joseph, 22, 61
Lasswell, Harold D., 76
League of Catholic Action (France),
  38
League of Colored Peoples (B), 41
League of Women Voters of the
  United States, 42
Lee, Ivy, 68
Leibniz, 4
LeMay, General Curtis, 52
Liberal party (B), 21

Liberal party (Sweden), and white-
  collar workers, 22
Lipset, Seymour Martin, 59, 60
Lobby, 2, 13, 16, 17, 19
Lobby-agent, 9n, 13, 19
Lobbyer, 13
Lobbying:
  in Bryce, Lane, 1–2
  stimulated by congressional
    committee system, 53
Lobbyist, 9n, 13, 17, 19
Lobby-member, 9n, 13, 19
London Foundation for Marriage
  Education, 39
London Rubber Industries, 39

McKean, Dayton David, 99
Mackenzie, W. J. M., 2
Maine, Sir Henry, 28
Massel, Mark S., 64
"Mental experiment," 8
Merton, Robert K., 100
Meynaud, Jean, 44
Milbrath, Lester, 16
Mill, John Stuart, 3, 27
Ministry of Agriculture (B), 67
Ministry of Aviation (B) (*see* Ministry
  of Technology)
Ministry of Pensions (B), 90
Ministry of Technology (B), 51, 52n
Ministry of Transport (B), 53, 92
Motor Agents' Association (B), 92
"Mr. Cube" campaign (B), 70, 71
Mulder, Mauk, 84

National American Woman Suffrage
  Association, 41–42
National Anti-Vivisection Society (B),
  43
National Association for the
  Advancement of Colored
  People, 26
National Association of Letter
  Carriers, 26
National Association of
  Manufacturers, 37, 39, 40, 68,
  71, 72, 81, 90, 93
National Economic Development
  Council (B), 25
National Farmers Union, 97
National Farmers' Union (B), 40, 89
National Federation of Business and
  Professional Women's Clubs,
  38

National Federation of Pakistani
　　Associations (B), 41
National Industrial Council, 39
National Industrial Recovery Act, 68
National Labor Relations (Wagner)
　　Act, 68, 69
National Liberal Federation (B), 21
National Metal Trades Association, 81
National Petroleum Council, 63, 91
National Production Authority, 62, 63
National Rural Letter Carriers, 26
National Society for Clean Air (B), 43
National Society for the Prevention
　　of Cruelty to Children, Inc.
　　(B), 43
National Union of Women Teachers
　　(B), 38
New Zealand Employers' Federation,
　　37
Nominal definition (see Definition)
Norris–La Guardia Act, 1932, 81

Odegard, Peter, 22
Oil Industry Information Committee,
　　72
Organized group, 1, 2, 16

"Parallelism," 50
Parsons, Talcott, 28, 33, 34, 35
Partito Comunista Italiano, 22
Partito Socialista Italiano, 22
Pattern-maintenance and tension-
　　management, as pattern
　　variable, 33, 95
"Pattern-variables," 29, 45
"Peak" organizations, 37, 38, 68
Pennsylvania Society for the
　　Encouragement of Manufacturers
　　and the Mechanic Arts, 10
Philadelphia Society for the
　　Promotion of National
　　Industry, 10
Political culture (see Culture,
　　political)
Political group, 18
Political interest group, 1, 17
Political science:
　　action, not acts, basic "units" of, 8
　　and historical method, 80n
　　meanings approach, 6–8, 7n, 27,
　　　31, 36, 38, 44, 47
　　not confined to observables, 7
Potter, Allen, 2
Poujadism, 21

Power:
　　as coercive influence, 76
　　common concept, 74
　　in Derthick, 74–75
　　in Locke, 75n, 76
Pressure group:
　　in Hunt, Reynaud, Anderson, 1–2
　　as name, 17, 19
Pressure Politics, 17
Prestige association, exemplified, 35
Primary group (see Group, social)
Prime Minister (B), and British
　　Legion, 42
Prince of Wales, rebuked by King
　　George V, 42
Private government, 24
Private organization, 1, 2, 16
Prohibition Amendment, 40
Public interest, 87, 90–91
Public Relations (see also
　　Advertising, political)
　　concept:
　　　advertising, 50
　　　origin of, 67
　　a definition, 67
　　induced by "parallelism," 50, 52
　　in long run, 67–72
　　　American firms, 67–69, 72
　　　British firms, 69–72
　　in short run, 51–53, 55

Racial Adjustment Action Society
　　(B), 41
Real definition (see Definition)
Reynaud, Jean-Daniel, 2
Riggs, Fred W., 2
Road Haulage Association (B), 70, 90,
　　92
Roads Campaign Council (B), and
　　road program, 92
Robinson, Richard, 3, 3n
Roosevelt, President Franklin, 63, 68
Rose, Richard, 59
Royal Horticultural Society (B), 35
Royal Society for the Prevention of
　　Cruelty to Animals (B), 43
Ruth, Babe, 78

Sartori, Giovanni, 3n
Scottish Society for the Protection of
　　Wild Birds, 43
Secondary group (see Group, social)
Secrétariat d'Etude pour la Liberté
　　de l'Enseignement et la
　　Défense de la Culture, 40, 43

"Self-contained" flow (see Influence, flows of)
Shared-attitude group (see Attitude group)
Shils, Edward A., 54
Simmel, Georg, 89, 89n
"Simplex" flow (see Influence, flows of)
Simpson, George E., 25
Soap Makers Federation (B), 96
Social deference, 57, 58n
Social Democratic Federation (B), 20–21
Social Democratic Party (Sweden), and Federation of Labor, 22
Social organization (see Social system)
Social structure (see Social system)
Social system:
  collective arrangements, 32
  secondary groups:
    dysfunctional for, 35
    functional for, 35–36
    latently functional for, 36, 41
Society of Motor Manufacturers and Traders (B), 92
Standard Oil Company, 68
"Status to Contract," 28
Stichting voor de Landbouw (Netherlands), 37
Strauss, G. R., 92n
Streat, Sir Raymond, 91, 92
Structural functionalism, 31
Study association, defined and exemplified, 35
Styles of action:
  and comparability of interest-groups, 78, 79n, 102
  immediate determinants:
    distinguished from ultimate, 45–46
    listed, 46–47
    in long run, 62–72
    in short run, 48–62 (a first approximation, 48–55; a closer approximation, 55–56; reducibility to "political culture" variable, 56–62)
  and net endowments, 50
Sutton, Francis X., 29, 30, 31
Synthesis:
  as kind of real definition, 4, 5
  as real definition of interest-group, 27–30

Target:
  defined, 15, 24
  intermediate, 24
  meaning to Actor, 44
  selected by Actor, 47
  terminal, 24
    private, 24
    public, 24
Tawney, R. H., 43, 74
Taylor, A. J. P., 80n
Tennessee Valley Authority, 67
TFX aircraft (F-111), 49n, 53
Thayer, George, 43
Thomas, Sir Miles, 50
Tivey, Leonard, 92
Tönnies, Ferdinand, 28
Tocqueville, de, 56, 57
Truman, David, 2, 17, 43n, 54
Truman, President, 98
TSR-2 aircraft, 49n

"Uncle Abner Says," 68
Union de Défense des Commerçants et des Artisans (Poujadist), 21
Union Française des Associations de Combattants et Victimes de la Guerre, 42
Union et Fraternité Française (Poujadist), 21
Union "peaks," Italian, and parties, 22
Union of Soviet Socialist Republics, interest-groups in, 100–101
Union of Women Painters and Sculptors (France), 42
United Federation of Postal Clerks, 26
United States Brewers' Association, 17
United States Chamber of Commerce, 37, 72, 98
United States Supreme Court, as interest-group Target, 25–26
United States Temperance Union, 10
Universal Colored People's Association (B), 41

Verba, Sidney, 59
Veterans Administration, 67
Vose, Clement, 26

Wahlke, John, 87, 88
Wales, Prince of, rebuked by King George V, 42
Weber, Max, 8

Western Electric Company, 51, 66
West Indian Standing Conference
    (B), 41
Wheare, Sir Kenneth, 56
White-collar workers, Swedish, and
    Liberals, Conservatives, 22
Wilson, Charles E., 96
Wilson J. Cook, 4
Wilson, Woodrow, 53

Windsor, Duke of (see Wales, Prince
    of)
Wohlegemuth, Ernest, 92
Women's Social and Political Union
    (B), 41–42
World Council of Churches, 24
Wright, Representative James, 52

Yinger, J. Milton, 25